CHRISTMAS BRANCHES

JACK KLINE

CHRISTMAS BRANCHES

Available via Amazon.com and other bookstores. For reviews, permissions, large orders, and other inquiries, please contact:

Freeman Publishing Co.
PO Box 1294
Novi, MI 48376
FreeManPubCo@protonmail.com

Printed in the United States of America (2019)
ISBN 9781702100069

FREE MAN
PUBLISHING CO.

DEDICATION

*To the memory of Norm Ledgin (1928-2019),
the most Christian atheist I've ever known*

and to my dad.

"And it was always said of him, that he knew how to keep Christmas well, if any man possessed the knowledge. May that be truly said of us, and all of us!"

— Charles Dickens, *A Christmas Carol*

Acknowledgments

Since almost the beginning Priscilla Myers has been my confidant, advisor, and line-edit nitpicker. She also serves as cheerleader and dance team. And to heap one additional accolade, credit Prissy—a slam-bang photographer—for the gorgeous cover photo.

Norm Ledgin added advice to every story since 2010. Norm was a great man and a fine writer. He was my friend. I will miss him. Along with Norm, I thank the rest of our writer's posse: Pam, Theresa, Beth, Mike, and our new kid, Katie. My family, Nancy, Rebecca, and Conor provided heart, warmth, and humor to these stories, and much of the specific fodder for "Oh! Christmas Tree" and "Winter Wonderland."

The family I grew up with—my parents and siblings, my uncles-and-aunts' families, and my grandparents—all provided mostly joyful memories to the boy who dreamed up tales of Christmas. The Overland Park Christian Church, and Reverend Forrest Haggard gave the boy his foundation of faith. The boy and the man he became, who, together dreamed of Christmas and its many stories, thank all of those who contributed. And special thanks to my boyhood friend, Brian Wright, who constructed this volume and everything the process entails, then published it under his umbrella, *Free Man Publishing, Inc.*

Most of all, I want to thank Nancy, my wife of almost forty years—that's a lot of Christmases. She put up with a long list of foibles even before I began to write, and afterward the list grew longer. Though vastly different in so many ways we are two well-fitted gloves. When I think back on all of the gifts God has given me, Nancy may be the greatest.

Foreword

When I first began writing around fifteen years ago, I used my early stories to unmask emotions I have found difficult to express as one in a long line of stoic Kline men. Fiction made it easier to navigate my feelings. One of my earliest stories was about a painful Christmas when I was thirteen. This collection grew from that story, though I never dreamed of such a result.

The Kline family in which I grew up gradually built a load of holiday traditions that my brother, sister, and I loved. On Christmas when I was thirteen our father failed to meet his designated role in procuring the family tree. My siblings and I shamed him by taking on the task. In doing so we hurt him. Christmas festivities that year went on in pseudo normalcy, but he was unusually quiet and never fully participated. My part in that self-centered Christmastime slight lurked inside me for decades, though I never mentioned it to my dad.

In 2007 I wrote a story, "Naming Christmas," as an apology, as a way to excise my personal holiday demon. In it, the Larson family did what the Kline family should have done on that Christmas so long ago. I felt better after writing it. I even printed copies, slid them into Christmassy red folders and gave them as gifts to my family and extended family, including my dad.

Ironically, my dad did not remember that Christmas at all. But in our subsequent discussion I learned that there was one Christmas around then—it must have been the one—that because of a recession and some poor business choices he was in danger of losing his civil-engineering business, and even worse. It's funny, my fictionalized apology brought out a confession that he, being a stoic Kline man, had kept to himself for decades.

The next year for the holidays, I rewrote the first story of any kind I had ever written—for Mr. Beal in ninth-grade English—about a man saved from a frozen death in a Christmas Eve blizzard by Santa Claus, who happened to be flying overhead. "Only a Christmas Story" became a holiday gift to my family.

The bug had bitten. Each year since I have gifted my family a new story. A few have since been published, including "Christmas with the Pack" in the United Kingdom's *Prole* magazine. All of them up through 2018 are included in this collection.

Why *Christmas Branches* as the title?

Decorated evergreens were originally part of pagan celebrations of Winter Solstice. Gradually, particularly during Queen Victoria's reign in England, evergreens became integral in the Christian observation of Christmas. Each story in this volume is intended to be a branch of the overarching Christmas story—a story of joy, giving, faith, and love.

I hope readers feel how much I love Christmas and the magical feeling it engenders, both religious and secular. Some of these stories do not directly relate to the reason for the holiday, but they show warmth and generosity that are part of the season. And some reflect more directly on the birth of Christ, including an unusual visit to Bethlehem at the time Joseph went up from the town of Nazareth.

May these stories enhance your joy of this most special season.

Merry Christmas,

Jack
Louisburg, Kansas

Contents

Only a Christmas Story

I don't expect anyone to believe this story. I know I would not. I would say it was a bunch of hooey, or that the teller was playing me for a nincompoop, or maybe he had thrown down too many mugs of Christmas spirit. The tale is true enough. I know. I lived it. But, as Poe wrote in one of his scary stories: "I neither expect nor solicit belief. Mad indeed would I be to expect it in a case where my very senses reject their own evidence." So let's merely call it a Christmas story and leave it at that.

I drove west on Interstate 70 outside of Topeka, Kansas, a few hours before dark on Christmas Eve last year. As my PT Cruiser rolled past the Alma exit, I figured it was about nine hours to Boulder under normal circumstances. Circumstances were far from normal. Light snow had been falling since the 23rd and now it came down harder. The roads were slick and traffic crept. My flight from Kansas City to Denver had been a casualty. Once the flight was cancelled, I would have curled up with my Makers Mark and a procession of Christmas movies on television were it not for my kids, Travis and Norah.

Instead, I plodded into a sun muted and almost obliterated by the storm. This drive marked the second Christmas since my divorce. Lorraine and I weren't getting along that well before I slept with Sarah from the office. She meant nothing to me, or I to her, other than a foolish fling. Sarah might have been a last straw for Lorraine, or merely an excuse for the both of us to cut our losses. Unfortunately Travis, then only seven, and three-year-old Norah were living symbols of the loss cutting that came due. After the divorce, it tore me apart seeing them only every other weekend and for two weeks that summer. I found a place two miles from our family's house in Boulder, and knowing they were that

1

close and that some judge said I couldn't see them began carving an ulcer in me. So last year when I had a chance to transfer to Kansas City, to our Sprint corporate office, I leaped at the opportunity, hoping distance would ease the pain. It did not. But with a beefed up travel allowance, I saw them almost as often living in KC as I had in Boulder.

Lorraine was not the bad guy here. She worked with me to make sure I had every opportunity to be a real father. Roles reversed, I'm not sure I would have done the same. Last year Lorraine arranged for me to have the kids at my parent's house for five days beginning at 6:00 on Christmas night. My folks lived in Nederland, about twenty miles up the canyon from Boulder and we looked forward to having Travis and Norah for that long weekend. Snow storms might ground Southwest Airlines, but they wouldn't stop me. I had twenty-eight hours to make the nine hour drive and I planned to take it slow and steady, like that tortoise raced the hare.

The flakes swelled in size and I switched my wipers from intermittent to slow-and-steady. My Cruiser climbed into the Flint Hills, some of the most beautiful country on earth—rolling, treeless, and gorgeous—even in a snowstorm. One can see for miles in any direction with nary a house or a tree and precious few fences. It's like driving into another century. Cresting each rise allows for the expectation that some huge herd of bison, backs and massive shoulders covered with a layer of snow, might stand grazing silently in the valley below. I love the Flint Hills anytime. They are magical in the snow.

Surprisingly, only a few fools accompanied me as I passed the Junction City exit. I guess every sane person was with family, about to sit down to Christmas Eve dinner. It allowed me to hug the center stripe and avoid the drifts beginning to form on the north side of the slow lane since the last plow's passage. I daydreamed a bit. I viewed myself on the couch with the kids, reading them our traditional Christmas story. Norah, now old enough to read along, ensconced on my lap in her Christmas sweater, the red hair bow tickling my nose as I read. In my daydream, Travis lounged on the couch next to us pretending to be aloof, pretending to be too old. I remembered the previous year as the first year I did not spend Christmas or read a story to them. The divorce fresh, that holiday stood as a nightmare. I hoped they thought nothing of my failure to be with them two years ago, and that they had not missed our Christmas story. No, I hoped they had. The kids were older, Travis almost ten, and I had a volume of O. Henry short stories in the back with the presents and I thought this year I'd read "The Gift of the Magi." Maybe I'd ask Travis to trade off, to share the reading. The radio brought me out of my reverie.

I remember now how my heart seemed to stop dead last year when the radio announced that Interstate 70 was closing between Hays, Kansas and Limon, Colorado. Steering with my knees, a pretty intelligent thing to do in what was now being called a blizzard, I pulled maps out of the glove box and clicked on the map light. I looked for an alternate route, occasionally glancing up at the road in the dying light so I would have a slight advance warning of when I might be dying. I found what I was looking for. At Hays, I would dip down on US 183 to 96 and take it west to Limon. This would add hours to the trip, but I was in tortoise mode anyway. I put the maps on the passenger seat and flipped off the map light and repaid attention to the road. An hour later the Cruiser rolled into Hays. By then, the drifting snow, several inches deep, had covered about half of the slow lane and we few fools had trudged along in the misnomered fast lane. I exited at 183 and turned south through Hays where I stopped at a Casey's, topped off the tank, filled my Coleman thermos with coffee, and picked up a box of day-old donuts.

By dark, the strengthening wind made the snow seem to defy gravity. It no longer fell, but merely blew sideways across Kansas on its way to Oklahoma and Arkansas. They say Kansas is the third windiest state in the nation, but I don't believe it. There can't be two that are windier. Highway 96 began to drift in little stripes like waves on a decent-sized reservoir, and I pushed through them in my Cruiser as if I was busting across the wake of speedboaters. Between Ness City and Dighton the combination of the drifts and the wind had me floating all over the road. Luckily I averaged twenty-plus minutes between approaching vehicles, so I could hog the center line. Later that night, between eleven and midnight, somewhere outside of Tribune, I slid off the road and down an embankment.

It all seemed to play out in slow motion. I guess I must have hit a pretty big drift, which turned me a little sideways and I overcorrected. At that point, the steering wheel and the brakes were like one of those supermarket cars where the adult slides the quarter into the slot and the kid pretends to drive. That's what I did as I glided sideways towards the shoulder—pretended to drive. My Cruiser and I left the road and floated gently down the slope and into a deep drainage swale. We never slammed into anything, but came to a steady, gradual stop as if I had been in control the whole time. A couple of quick tries, reverse-forward-reverse convinced me that inertia held sway. I wasn't going anywhere without considerable help.

You don't grow up in Colorado without some knowledge of the dangers of driving in snow, and Lorraine and I had put together emergency kits for both cars. I shut off the engine, the headlights, and flipped on the overhead. The Cruiser's cargo space still held the mini duffel bag. I crawled back to the front, placed the duffel on top of my now useless maps and tried my Nextel, no reception, naturally. The duffel revealed two fat stubby candles, a smallish blanket, flashlight, a couple of those green light sticks, some match books in a moisture-proof plastic container and two coffee cans: one for the burning candle and one to melt snow for drinking water. The coffee that gurgled inside me sought escape so I pushed open the door, careful not to get a bunch of snow inside the car. I stepped out and went around to the back the car and urinated by the exhaust pipe, then pushed the snow away from the pipe so I could run the car for a few minutes without plugging up the exhaust. Retracing my steps, I kicked my boots against the side of the door, opened it and slid back in.

Once the car was heated and the engine shut off again, I lit a candle. They supplied a surprising amount of heat in a closed space I was told. I popped a light stick and placed it on the dash in hopes that someone driving by above might see it, and fetched my O. Henry book, opening it to "The Gift of the Magi." It sounds silly, but I read and rehearsed in the eerie light of candle and glow stick. I wanted so much to make those five days a golden time for the kids, a time to reconnect. Nothing less than a perfect reading would do. And reading O. Henry kept my mind off the possibility that I might be dead by morning. Dying by morning was a long shot as long as I was careful, but possible nonetheless.

So with the red wool blanket on my lap, I read "Gift" through twice, experimenting with delivery, tone and inflection. Then I moved on to other old favorites: "The Cop and the Anthem," "Memoirs of a Yellow Dog," and my favorite, "The Ransom of Red Chief." Somewhere in the middle of "Whistling Dick's Christmas Stocking" I fell asleep, which was not a terribly smart thing for one to do when snowbound and trying to survive. I don't know how long I slept. I awoke to a tapping on the passenger side window.

Sleepy and disoriented, it took me a few moments to

register where I was and what I was seeing. There was a man outside the window, glowing green. The light stick. The man wasn't green. He was smiling.

"Looks like you could use some help," he called out in a deep baritone.

"Yeah, hang on." I shed my grogginess and unlocked the door on his side. He opened it, lifted the maps and the duffel, sat down and swung the door shut.

"I saw your green glow from the highway. That was pretty sharp thinking. Looks like this car won't be going anywhere soon. Can I give you a lift?"

"Yeah, sure. I'm Jake Long." I offered him my hand and he grabbed it with near bone crushing vigor.

"Call me Nick." Nick looked maybe forty, and wore brown duck bibs over a red and black flannel shirt. He wore no coat. A St. Louis Cardinals ball cap was pulled down low over his eyes. "Pleased to meet you, Jake," he said, grinning through a well-trimmed salt and pepper goatee that partially obscured the beginnings of a double chin.

"Can you take me into the next town?"

"That's Tribune, Jake. Ain't nobody stirring there this time of night, nor probably on Christmas day either. I'm headed west."

"Where to?" I asked.

"All the way to Boulder, Colorado. I can take you that far if you like and you can call about the car on the 26th. Whatya say?"

"Well, I'm headed to Boulder myself."

"Don't that beat all," he said wearing an unreadable smile—as if he were hiding something. I thought of Stephen King for some reason, and how this guy might be some kind of real-life horror story. "Well, why don't you go ahead and secure this puppy and we'll get going. We're burning Christmas you know." He opened his door, slid out and replaced the maps and duffel on the seat. I blew out the candle and opened mine. The wind still blew hard and snow pellets stung my face. I reached in the back and grabbed my valise, stepped out and swung the door shut, sweeping a small part of the snow drift inside.

'Don't forget the presents and your book, Jake."

"Oh, yeah." I reopened the Cruiser, leaned into the back for my Target bag full of gifts, grabbed O. Henry off the console and slid it into the bag, and stepped back out. The car secured, I hefted my bags. "Lead on Nick."

"Here, let me carry that." He held out his hand for the valise.

"That's okay. I got it."

"No, I insist. That slope is a lot steeper than it looks, and it's slippery." He held his hand out like an adult waiting for a child and wiggled his fingers with impatience. I handed the valise to him and Nick threw it over his shoulder. "Let's hit it, Jake."

The slope was steep and slick, and even though we followed my now mostly obscured tire tracks, the snow lay deep. I followed in Nick's footsteps, my boots slipping and sliding. Nick wore some kind of Eskimoey mukluks with deep treads and his feet never faltered. How did he know about the presents and the book? I decided that the book was right there on the console. He could have seen it, and as for the presents, after all it was Christmas. The wind blew even stronger up on the highway. The cold penetrated. His car idled, duel exhaust plumes dissipating in the wind, promising warmth inside. It was an old roadster of some kind and sat low, sleek and dark, maybe black. The front wheels looked chrome and they set off wide white-walled tires. The rear wheels were obscured by fender skirts.

Nick walked around to the driver's side and his deep voice boomed over the wind's howl, "The door's unlocked." We opened ours simultaneously. Nick tossed the valise over the seat into the back and I did the same with my Target bag. In the glow of the dashboard, I noted the candy-cane rolled and pleated front seat. A pine-shaped air freshener hung from the rearview, spewing an aroma of deep woods. The car sported a floor-mounted stick shift with a bright-red shifter knob. The car was a beauty. Nick revved the engine. It rumbled—no stock engine under that hood.

"So what is this car, Nick, what make?"

"It's a '49 Mercury. They called the Mercurys from that era Lead Sleds cause they were so dang solid and heavy." He let out the clutch and after a moment of spinning motionlessness, the Mercury rolled forward, splaying the shoulder's snow and gravel.

"I hope you like Christmas music," he flipped down his sun visor pulled out a CD and inserted it into a modern stereo in the antique dashboard. Church bells began to clang, followed by whistles and violins.

"I do like Christmas music. What's this one? I don't recognize it."

"The Chieftains. It's Irish Christmas music."

"Don't think I've ever heard any, interesting."

"I love all kinds—Christmas all over the world—all different, all good." He smiled, and whistled along with what he later said were Uilleann pipes.

The Mercury—the Lead Sled—didn't seem to mind the drifting snow like my Cruiser had. It plowed through it as if the snow was that fluffy fake stuff they use in displays. Some of the bigger drifts poofed up around the front of the car, spraying the hood and windshield, leaving us sightless for a moment. Whereas I had been driving with muscles tense, shoulders and neck aching, ready for any eventuality and anticipating trouble, he seemed to be careless, almost flippant, like we were on a sunny Sunday drive in the country.

We talked some about baseball. I told him the Rockies and the hapless Royals were my teams, and as evidenced by his cap, he told me that he followed the Cards. Followed, put it mildly. I got the blow-by-blow of the current Cardinals strengths and weaknesses and Nick went into the proud history of the franchise as if he were trying to persuade me to switch allegiance. I heard about Musial and Gibson and Schoendienst. He told me of Grover Alexander's great comeback from alcoholism in 1926, and how with his fastball gone, he won the World Series for the Cards on guts alone, winning game six and saving game seven. And he knew everything about the '34 Cards, the famous Gashouse Gang, their tendencies, strengths, what kind of pitches Dizzy and Daffy Dean threw, even the player's nicknames: Ripper, Ducky, the Lip and more.

"Sounds almost like you were there—like you watched all those guys play."

"Just a student of the game," he said with a smile.

The sky lightened as we past the Colorado line, heralding the sun's impending arrival. As if in deference to the sun, the snow let up some, smaller flakes anyway. I noticed the hood ornament.

"That a deer?" I asked, pointing to the hood.

"Yep, an 18 point buck."

"You a hunter?"

"Heavens no," he laughed. "I just like animals, especially deer."

"That wouldn't be a reindeer would it?" I looked out my side window at the passing fence posts in the growing light. I was getting weirded out a little and couldn't look at him.

"Why do you ask?"

"Well," Now I turned to face him, I had to. "I was beginning to think maybe I was riding with Santa Claus."

He laughed loudly in that deep throaty voice—a Santa Claus laugh if I ever heard one.

"You got me, Jake. My secret's out. And as long as we're sharing secrets, you can fess up now too."

"What do you mean?"

"Fess up, Jake. I've known for a while now. You're the Easter Bunny," his laugh resounded. I smiled.

"So you're not Santa Claus?"

"I didn't say that. But I can see you're conflicted here. Let's just say that I'm a man who loves Christmas and who likes to have fun." He grinned at me for the longest time. I would say there was a twinkle in his eye, but I don't remember and I'd be embellishing just for the sake of the story. But he smiled at me, twinkle or no, for so long that I finally pointed to the highway reminding him that we *were* driving in a snowstorm. Nick laughed, turned his eyes to the road, and without looking, ejected The Chieftains and popped in another. This one I recognized. It was Reba McEntire singing "Away in the Manger."

Around 8:00 am we turned north on 287. The highway here was in much better shape. A snowplow had preceded us north not too long before.

"With any luck, we'll be in Limon by 10:00. You hungry?"

"I'm so hungry I could eat a reindeer," I said. Nick roared and I swear the inside of his car vibrated.

Once his laughter subsided, he responded, "We'll stop there and maybe eat something a little more traditional."

I must have dozed off soon after, because the next thing I knew we were pulling into Rip Griffins, a monster-sized truck stop in Limon where 24 and I-70 split, the former headed for Colorado Springs and the latter for Denver. The restaurant's foggy windows forecast a pleasant respite as we carefully navigated the patchy ice in the almost empty parking lot. Once inside, it was toasty and humid with the pungent aroma of bacon and coffee. A smattering of truckers spending Christmas on the road ate and drank coffee. Nick ordered a stack of buttermilk pancakes—he called them flapjacks—and I had biscuits and gravy with a side of bacon. We both ordered coffee and Nick told our waitress, Sylvia, to leave plenty of room for cream and sugar in his.

"I like my coffee as sweet as you are," he said, or something like that. Sylvia didn't seem to mind. They hit it off right away, and I will bet our coffee cups never got half empty. On one of her trips with the pot we chatted. She told us that her husband was in Iraq with his guard unit and her three kids, all under ten, were at her parents in Castle Rock. She had worked a double and was getting off at noon to join them. Sylvia started back to the counter when Nick caught her by her forearm. He leaned forward and whispered in her ear for a whole minute or more. Sylvia nodded several times and then her eyes lit up. She hugged him and kissed him on the cheek. "God bless you, Nick." He winked at me.

"What'd you say to her?"

"I just wished her a merry Christmas."

"The way you were going, I thought you would ask her to sit on your lap and tell you what she wanted for Christmas." Nick guffawed, and heads around the room lifted from their eggs and their coffee.

When Sylvia left the check, Nick and I argued good-naturedly about who would take care of it. We agreed to flip a coin and he pulled out a very old silver Peace dollar. He sent it spinning in the air.

"Call it."

"Tails," I said. He caught the coin, glanced at it surreptitiously, and stuck it back in his jeans.

"Nope, heads."

Nick left a fifty for what must have been a fifteen dollar ticket and slid his chair back. "I need to use the gentlemen's room and then we'll hit the road okay?" As he stood, he called out "Merry Christmas, Sylvia."

"Have a Merry Christmas, gents. And I won't forget what you told me, Nick. Thanks." She waved from behind the counter.

The wind had let up some, but the snow still fell moderately. The slow lane on I-70 west appeared to be in pretty good shape and the fast lane, though snowpacked, had been recently plowed. I tried to call Lorraine to ask if I could borrow her car to take the kids to my folks, but the battery was dead. Nick didn't carry one. He said we would make it to Lorraine's well before six and if I needed to, I could call my parents from there and have them come get me and the kids.

"Sounds like a plan." I told him.

He asked about my family and I opened to him. I told him about Lorraine and me, even about my affair. Nick focused his questions and interest on Travis and Norah. He couldn't get enough and told me the biggest regret he and his wife had was their inability to have kids.

"We love kids, Samantha and I. We like to think of ourselves as kind of second parents to every kid we know." He said this with a mixture of pride and longing, and seemed almost melancholy.

"I want you to meet Travis and Norah. When we get to Lorraine's place I'll introduce you. If it's okay with my folks, maybe you could come up to Nederland and have Christmas dinner with us—that is if you don't have other plans?" I observed him pondering as he drove. "So what about you, Nick? Are you on your way home?"

"Nope, not yet. I have some friends to visit first, but I'll be headed home directly." He smirked, and with his look, he invited interplay.

I obliged. "Home to the North Pole?"

"Ha," he chuckled and pointed at me. "I knew that was coming. You won't let it go. Lumps of coal in your stocking next year, young man." He let out a staged and artificial "Ho, Ho, Ho," but it sounded perfect, as if he had practiced it for hundreds of years.

"Still," I said, "if you really are him, you're either a terrible slacker or easily distracted, wasting most of your big night with me. And here it's almost noon on Christmas day and you are driving across eastern Colorado in a car for crying out loud."

"Santa wouldn't consider you a waste, Jake—a project maybe, but not a waste."

"Okay, but if he did spend most of the night before Christmas with me, billions of kids would get stiffed."

He laughed long and loud and I worried again that he had forgotten he was driving. Nick pulled out a white handkerchief and wiped his eyes, while I had my hand poised ready to grab the wheel. But the Mercury cruised along I-70 in the slow lane, perfectly centered, as if it had a mind of its own.

"What?" he said. "You don't think Santa can multi-task?" We laughed a duet—my baritone and his deeper one. Then he turned serious. "I believe that Santa Claus exists as a part of God's miracle, the miracle birth of the Child, his Son. If God wanted, Santa could be in a thousand, no, a million places at once—even driving down the highway in a really cherry '49 Mercury."

"Wait, you saying you *are* Santa Claus?"

"No, I'm just a man who loves..."

"...Christmas and likes to have fun," I finished for him, and I had to chuckle.

"Now you're cookin' with gas, Jake."

I changed the subject. "So, Nick, what do think? Would you like to have dinner with Travis, Norah and my folks?"

"Sorry, I'll have to take a rain check."

"Okay, but I'm gonna hold you to that," I said with mock sternness, then continued, "at least let me introduce you to the kids when we get to Lorraine's."

"I'd like that."

In Denver, the conditions on I-70 were a hundred times worse. That stretch of 70 through Denver is mostly bridge, or more succinctly 'raised highway.' But the fact is, there's no place to push the snow and a lot had fallen, too much to melt with salt. It had packed down hard, several inches thick in places. The lanes ran bumpy and rutted like some old heavily-used wagon trail. Traffic crawled, and Nick's Mercury, which might be called a low-rider, didn't care for it at all. Nick didn't seem to mind though. His spirits were high. He sang the song about chestnuts with Nat King Cole and then a perfectly pitched duet with Judy Garland on "Have Yourself a Merry Little Christmas." I joined in on the "through the years" chorus and we three sounded pretty good.

Once we got onto US 36, the roads were a little better and we picked up some speed. I told Nick to take the Broomfield exit. Thirty minutes later we were on the south edge of Boulder nearing Lorraine's house.

"I want to at least give you some money for gas, Nick."

He didn't take his eyes from the road. "Nope. Call it my Christmas present."

"But what about me? I haven't given you anything. You gave me a ride, maybe saved my life, and then wouldn't even let me pay for our meal. What about me?"

We were only a few blocks from Lorraine's but he pulled over to the curb, put the Mercury in neutral and pulled the emergency brake. He turned to face me.

"Jake, you gave me companionship on Christmas, on what would otherwise have been a lonely drive. That's something special. But if you really want to give me a gift for Christmas, here's what you do: love those kids, love them fiercely. Be the best dad you can be and don't just tell them what is right, show them. Be there for them, but most of all, make sure they never doubt your love.

"That's a tall order, I know," Nick paused. "But it would be a fitting gift even for Santa Claus." His eyes penetrated me and he offered no smile this time.

I felt kind of choked up, but managed, "I would be honored to fulfill that gift, Nick."

He turned back to the street, let off the brake, revved the engine and slipped the Mercury into gear.

A few minutes later, Nick pulled up to the curb across the street across from Lorraine's. He parked and left the car idling.

"Do you have time to come in and meet the kids?"

"If I go in, I'm afraid I won't be able to pry myself away and I really do need to be elsewhere. Why don't you bring them out to the car?"

"Okay," I said. "But I haven't forgotten you owe me a rain check on dinner."

I opened the door, leaned over the seat and grabbed the sack of gifts and my valise. As I walked around the back, I noticed the Mercury had Alaska plates. At the front door, I rang the bell and waited. I was about two hours early. A streak of light across the peephole and then the door swung open violently.

"Jake! My God, we thought you were dead!" It was Lorraine. She punched me in the chest with both fists and then hugged me with no small amount of ferocity.

"Your parents called. The Kansas Highway patrol phoned them, told them they had found your car buried in a snow drift, but there was no sign of you. They feared you had tried to walk to Tribune. We were frantic! Why didn't you call?" She let go of me, her eyes full of accusation.

"My phone was dead. I didn't..."

"Dad!" The kids stormed down the stairs and hit me like linebackers, bashing me back against the doorframe. They combined efforts to crush my rib-cage. I looked over their heads at Lorraine. She was crying. We all stood, frozen for a few moments.

"Hey everybody, there's someone I want you to meet. Travis, Norah, wait till you see his car. He's waiting out by the curb." I turned and Nick was gone: no car, no sound of exhaust rumbling away down the street, nothing. He had vanished.

"Okay, you just about had me," Larry said. We sat at the terminal bar at Kansas City International. Larry waited for his flight announcement to Pittsburgh and I waited for mine. He sipped his pale ale. "A pretty good tale though, I must admit. So, are you going to visit your kids in Boulder again this year?"

"Actually, I'm spending Christmas with Lorraine and the kids. Lorraine and I have been kind of dating some, and she invited me for the weekend and we're all going to my folks for Christmas dinner. All the Southwest flights are a little backed up and, like you, I'm just waiting for my flight."

"Hey that's great. I hope things work out for you. You never heard from that weird Santa Claus guy again?"

"Well, I did get a Christmas card from Nick last week."

"Son-of-a-gun, are you serious?"

"Yeah, a beautiful card, the manger scene. On the inside at the bottom he wrote: *Merry Christmas to you and yours, Jake. I haven't forgotten the rain check I owe you, and I would love to meet your kids. Who knows, maybe this Christmas at Lorraine's in Boulder...*"

"All right, now you're pulling my leg. So what was the return address, the North Pole?" Larry drained his beer and collected his belongings.

"No return address. But, the envelope was postmarked Point Barrow, Alaska." Larry laughed at that and stood.

"Well Jake, my flight's about to board. It was a pleasure meeting you. And I enjoyed your story but I'm afraid I just ain't buying it." He offered his hand and I shook it. Larry turned and started to walk toward his gate when he stopped abruptly and spun around. "Wait a second. If you haven't seen him, how did he know you would be at your wife's for Christmas?"

"You tell me Larry."

"Oh no. No way. I'm not some fish you can hook and then reel in. Nice try, but I still don't believe you." He gave me a salute and turned to go.

16

"Hey, that's okay, really, it is," I called out and he paused again. "I neither expected nor solicited belief, remember? It was only a Christmas story." I waved to him as he hurried down the corridor.

The Flyover

"He's not real. Santa Claus is just a miff," Holly explained to my sister and me. She was only six years old. How could a six-year old give up on Santa Claus? That's the way I remember it anyway. Age softens people's memories, and details grow a layer of fuzz with time. But let me tell it the way I remember it, and understand that the story itself happened, if perhaps not in the exact detail I shall relate.

When I was growing up, every Christmas Eve my Uncle Jim and my Aunt Robin came to dinner. Uncle Jim was my mom's kid brother. My sister, Judith and I actually enjoyed the visit once Holly was born. Before Holly, we dressed up for inspection, got our cheeks pinched while they exclaimed how much we had grown, and then we remained in "best behavior mode" until time to clear dinner plates. Once dinner was finished, the grown-ups moved into the kitchen to slug down a handful of cocktails as they listened to the sounds of Christmas music on my parents' Magnavox.

Until Holly was born Judith and I lounged on the davenport and watched the sappy old Christmas shows like Rudolph and Frosty and Charlie Brown while the adults accomplished their imbibing. At nine, the grownups would lug their drinks in for Perry Como's Christmas show. They chatted through the whole show, with Aunt Robin by then slurring her words. But when Perry Como sang a carol, as if by some unseen secret adult code, they all quieted and their eyes grew rapt with Como's Christmas spirit. I must admit, that cat could croon a Christmas carol. After Como's show, my uncle and aunt donned coats and headed for the door, which was about fifteen feet away. Those fifteen feet were like the Bataan death march; each year it must have averaged a full thirty minutes. Judith and I didn't mind, because as soon as the march concluded we were to be sent to bed. Let them take all night we opined.

Once Holly was born, Christmas Eve became about her for a couple of years. We all marveled at the little babe, and my parents joined in their own cheek-pinching, "how-she's-grown," "isn't she cute" ritual. Judith was nine when Holly was born, and I was nearly seven. By the time Holly crawled and had begun her pre-walking, pulling-herself-to-her-feet stage, the grownups merely marveled at her, up until dinner. Afterward, she was left to her own devices in the care of her cousins. I have to say, Holly provided more fun for my sister and me than any Christmas toy or game during her toddler years.

At the exact moment of her authoritative Santa bombshell we were building small Lincoln log towns in order that Holly's stuffed elephant might rampage thru them, destroying buildings and flattening the town's army-man populace. This construction/demolition game had been a favorite Christmas Eve pastime for our band of three during these last two Christmases. Charlie Brown was hauling a scrawny little tree across the screen of our black and white Zenith as our construction process completed. Randy the Republican elephant—as Judith and I had dubbed him—stomped through the army-man village under the direction of Holly's right hand. While Randy romped, Judith in passing asked Holly if she was excited about Santa Claus coming soon. That's when she laid the "Santa is not real—just a miff" on us. After speaking, Holly set Randy down in the town square and inhaled deeply. She seemed sad but resigned, and wise beyond her six years.

"Who told you that?" my sister asked.

"Andrew, and he's in the second grade so he knows."

"And who told Andrew such a thing?" I asked.

"I don't know, but his mommy said it was true."

Judith asked her if she had talked to *her* parents about it. Holly told us that she just found out two days ago and she was afraid to talk to them. I asked her why.

"Because Andrew says that the parents are the ones who are playing a trick on the kids. They pretend that Santa comes, but really it's just them. Andrew's parents said so," Holly sighed. "They told him that Santa was real a long time ago but then he died and all of the parents made him into a miff."

"Myth," my sister corrected.

"Yes, mifth." Her eyes held a glimmer of hope, as if she wanted to believe that the knowledgeable second-grader might have made a mistake. We seized on that glimmer.

"Andrew is wrong," Judith said.

"But his parents..."

"He's wrong and I don't know why his parents told him that. Santa was born a long time ago, but he's still alive and hard at work every Christmas," Judith said.

Holly looked skeptically at my sister, the same look Natalie Wood gave Edmund Gwen in *Miracle on 34th Street*. "How do you know?" she asked.

"Because we've seen him," I blurted out. Judith's expression made it clear that was not the tactic she had in mind.

"You have not. When?" Holly's look changed in those four words from one of reproach to one of interest. And Judith's expression told me that the ball was in my court. We all waited to see the next gem that would come spewing from the synapses of my almost thirteen-year-old brain. And it took a while for the cranial spew to reach my mouth.

"When I was almost your age, Judith and I were playing in her room on Christmas Eve and listening to the carols on WHB. From the station we heard a report that Santa Claus had been picked up on radar near Kansas City." Both girls eagerly listened, Judith with one eyebrow raised. Even Randy, the Republican elephant leaned in my direction.

"You see, Santa will never stop at a house until everyone is sleeping. And he can't wait around until everyone falls asleep everywhere to get started. So, he hops around all over the world as soon as it gets dark. He might come to Kansas City three times in one night to give presents to the ones who go to sleep early first, and then come back for the others later." I had them. Judith smiled.

"So when we heard that he had been spotted over Kansas City, Judith and I went to her bedroom window. At first there was nothing, but then we heard sleigh bells jingle. And still we saw nothing." I paused, stretching the moment.

"The bells got louder. And that's when we saw Santa Claus fly over in his sleigh. We didn't see any red-nosed reindeer, but then it was a clear night. You remember don't you Judith?"

Holly turned her head to my sister. Judith nodded. "Yes, I do. I'll never forget that night."

Holly's eyes brightened, and for a moment we had given her back her Santa Claus. My mom must have just taken sugar cookies out of the oven and their aroma added to our victory. But Holly's face darkened, her lips crinkled, making her mouth look too tiny for her face.

"Andrew warned me that grownups would lie to try and keep the mifth alive."

"Hey, we're not grownups," I said.

"Greg's right," Judith said. "We're just big kids."

"You're almost grownups. And I don't think it's true. You didn't see him because he's not real. You're just being nice."

The television began Burl Ives' Frosty story and we had reached a stalemate. Precocious Holly at best sat on the fence now, not fully unbelieving but unwilling to buy into this particular Christmas miracle. Holly and

Randy continued their rampage through the little town and Judith and I were left to our private thoughts. My synapses fired up again. A plan sprouted and grew branches like some time-lapse accelerated pine seedling at Grower's Christmas tree farm.

I walked into the kitchen, grabbed a sugar cookie off the pan and stuffed it whole into my mouth before my mother could get up and swat my fingers. Instead I got a stern "no more" as she explained what I already knew—the cookies were to take to my grandparents on Christmas Day. A suitable amount of time wasted, I returned to the family room. Frosty was in big trouble on the tube, but we already knew that he would return again someday. The village lay in ruins and Randy napped nearby.

"Judith, mom wants us to go to the basement and get her some stuff," I announced. Judith's eyebrows raised and I jerked my head back towards the basement steps beyond the kitchen. She nodded. Holly lived in mortal fear of our dingy basement, as did I when I was her age. "Why don't you stay here and rebuild the village, Holly." She cheerfully obliged.

In the basement I presented my plan. Judith would take Holly to play in her room. Our family has some authentic sleigh bells that we hang from the ceiling beam between the family room and the kitchen each Christmas. They hang down and people—mostly but not solely kids—tap them as they walk through, exhibiting their Christmas spirit. At precisely 8:10, I would put a coat on, get a chair from the dining room and quietly unhook the bells. Then I would slip outside and around to the side of the house, near, but out of sight of Judith's window. I'd rhythmically begin shaking the bells. Judith would look at Holly, exclaim something like "Do you hear that?" and away to the window she would fly in a flash with Holly right behind her. Judith would point and profess to see Santa. And we'd let Holly's young imagination take it from there.

As I laid it out, Judith's grin grew larger. "Perfect, little brother, perfect," she said, and gave me a big hug even though I was way too old for them.

As eight o'clock approached Judith took Holly into her room to play dolls. Much as I loved twisting dolls heads off, I told them no thanks when they asked me to join. It was almost time to put my coat on and grab the bells when the parents strolled out of the kitchen, through the dining room and began a slow march towards the door. It seems that Uncle Jim had a nice bottle of champagne at home that he was about to fetch. They lived only eight blocks away, but their drink-in-hand procession to the door lingered interminably. At 8:10 I called Judith to her bedroom door and with softened voice apprised her of the delay. I told her that as soon as Uncle Jim leaves, and the gang goes back to the kitchen, I would hurry out and shake the bells loudly. We agreed on the revised plan.

The parents, however, marched in molasses. I began to have my doubts that the door would be reached and opened before the clock struck midnight. Frantically I tried to devise a way to speed the march. Nothing came to mind. My brain had already fulfilled its daily quota of scheming. I sat on the davenport, Frosty was a mere puddle of his former self when the television began to hawk the latest offerings from Mattel. My foot, with a mind of its own, tapped incessantly.

The door to Judith's bedroom burst open. Holly came screaming toward us.

"Mommy, Daddy, we just saw Santa Claus!" She smacked into her mother's legs, sloshing Aunt Robin's drink onto her red Christmas sweater. "We heard his sleigh bells and we opened the window and there he was. He flew right over us!"

Judith looked at me and winked. Now all of the grownups said grown-uppy things to her about how exciting that was, and how special, and didn't she know that he wouldn't come to her house until she was fast asleep—some crafty adult ammunition to get her to settle down later. Holly's spirits soared with her new favorite lively old elf, and all of the adults wore their own smiles of remembrance. Judith's grin covered her whole face.

Things calmed down and Uncle Jim went off for the champagne. Holly settled into her mother's lap on the davenport as we each found a spot for Perry Como. Uncle Jim returned and my mom got out her fancy champagne glasses. I got my first sip of champagne— yuck. Como's show was his best Christmas show ever. His guests, Rosemary Clooney and Dean Martin, gathered with him at the end for *Have Yourself a Merry Little Christmas* and there wasn't a dry eye in our house—except for Holly's which were closed. She slept soundly with her sugarplums.

After everyone had left, Judith and I prepared for bed. She came into my room, stepping around my scattered Civil War soldiers. Judith hugged me.

"You should have seen it Greg. It worked perfectly. You rang the bells and we ran to the window and opened it. I pointed to the sky. And she saw him instantly. And her enthusiasm was so contagious I almost thought I saw him too. Great job, Greg, and a really great idea!"

"I didn't do anything, Judith."

"Don't be modest, Greg. It was all your idea," my big sister said.

"No Judith, I'm serious. I didn't do anything. Everyone was bunched around the door. I couldn't get the sleigh bells. I didn't even go outside."

I'll never forget the look she gave me. Her mouth dropped open and I thought I saw the beginnings of tears, but her eyes spoke wonderment. And then she hugged me again—hard.

Christmas with the Pack

Previously published by *Prole Magazine,* United Kingdom

Brady Kirby wrote horror, pretty damn good horror. And he raked in a sizeable income from the sale of his books, not Stephen King or Dean Koontz income, but sizeable nonetheless. Lately the ladies and gentlemen of the press had dubbed him, along with the others, The Three K's of Horror. And scary book fans had picked up their lead. When they used the 3K phrase, sometimes they thought of King first and sometimes Koontz, but Kirby always came third. He was okay with that, just as he was fine with living alone in his five-bedroom home on the large wooded acreage between Beagle and Osawatomie, Kansas. The kids were grown and on their own, Ben nearby in Kansas City and Katie a senior at UCONN. His wife, Tanya had left him four years ago when Katie first went off to college. He liked the quiet. It facilitated his writing and beat the hell out of listening to Tanya bitch all of the time.

Tanya said he had become distant, whatever the hell that meant. She said that writing horror was changing him, and he remembered how pissed she got when he laughed, pulled out his pocket spiral and the slid the pencil off his ear saying, "Great story idea, Tawn. Writer turns evil writing evil stories. Thanks." As he scribbled on the spiral, she had pulled out an old first edition of *Messianic Man* from '87 and flung it at him. Brady easily ducked the 300 page missile and watched it smack the far bookshelf, dropping near his feet. 'Well, at least you have good taste, my first bestseller.'

That was almost four years ago. Occasionally he missed her and he still saw the kids now and then. Living alone, his writing had skyrocketed to a new level and his success, critically and monetarily, had notched up a bit closer to the other K's. His latest novel had actually gotten a good review from the *New York Times*, a Kirby first.

He didn't mind spending the holidays 'home alone' and thus far had never taken Tanya up on her annual 'Christmas day dinner with the kids' offer at her place in the KC suburb of Shawnee, an hour away. Last year he wrote the better part of his bestseller *The Witch of Windham Hill* between Christmas Eve and New Year's. Something about the time of year—the woods full of skeletonized trees except for the interloper cedars, the cold and the piles of dead leaves—lent itself to stirring creative juices. The fact that it was Christmastime surprisingly aided his ability to write horror. The dead of winter battling the promise of Christmas—that struggle, though all in his head, kept furious fingers flying across his Dell keyboard. Tonight, the night of the twenty-third, Christmas Eve-Eve his mother used to call it, he worked doggedly on the long anticipated sequel to *Messianic Man*.

His first bestseller had been about a man who worked 'miracles' and preached love and who many thought was the flesh-and-blood second coming of Jesus Christ. Just as many others, the Biblical book of *Revelation* fanatics believed him to be the *Anti*-Christ. Kirby had kept his readers in the dark, twisting his story both directions, and even a third, that his *man* might be a colossal con man. The book's culmination satisfied few, including many critics. Was he or wasn't he never was resolved, and the forces trying to destroy him or re-crucify him, depending on one's outlook, may or may not have succeeded. The body was never found; the figurative stone rolled away. *Messianic Man* made it to number seven on the *Time's* bestseller list that year, a few notches behind King's *Misery* and Koontz's *Watchers*. Those who read *Man* expected and anticipated a sequel. Some critics demanded it. Kirby could never abide demands. One might ask his parents, if they still lived, or certainly Tanya, who would vouch for his aversion to taking orders.

Now, twenty-two years later, the clamoring was only a memory, as a string of fourteen successful novels kept his readers blissfully occupied with almost annual rations of goosebumps.

The sun would set soon and Kirby decided to take a break. He shook his wrists as he strode into the kitchen, too many hours at the keyboard always went after his wrists first. Kirby pulled a pack of Buddig corned beef out of the fridge, tore off the end and slapped the entire eight ounce pack onto a slice of forty-five calorie diet wheat. He added a slice of fat-free sharp cheddar and rolled it up—his meat-heavy, diet-conscious version of dinner—after all, he had to work on his growing paunch. Kirby put on his insulated Carhartt, grabbed his gloves, a can of Diet Coke and headed out the kitchen door.

He would take a walk in the woods and maybe burn most of the calories he was consuming. As soon as Kirby stepped outside he heard the coyotes, the blessed coyotes. His neighbor, a half mile down the gravel road, hated the coyotes, but he loved them. The neighbor kept chickens and Kirby supposed he would feel differently if coyotes pilfered his coop. But he loved their frequent serenades, their eight- and ten-part harmonies. Coyotes were wary of man, and cohabited nicely so long as you weren't raising small livestock. Tonight their music soared, better to his mind than the tired Como, Crosby and Mathis carols on the Sirius radio inside.

His jerk neighbor down the road had initiated a campaign against Kirby's canine friends—had tried to enlist him. Kirby not only told him no, but told him that he would call the Miami County Sheriff if he set traps, or even set foot on Kirby's land. Old man Martin had even taken to hanging coyote skins from the oak branches on his drive, Kirby guessed as a warning to the pack, or more likely as a way to flaunt his success every time Kirby drove in to Osawatomie.

Light snow floated aimlessly in the porch light as he stood listening to the canine chorus. In the distance, he could hear Frank Martin's worthless Labrador join in. The lab actually sounded pretty good and he wondered if the dog might be happier out with the coyotes. Scattered, nickel-sized snowflakes fell in the windless cold as he set out into the woods. He found one of the familiar deer trails that led down to the creek in the south draw. The coyotes ceased their hallelujah chorus—they must be nearby and aware. Maybe they intuited the Martin-Kirby boundary and kept their base of operations safe on his land.

The trail tracked down through the oak and cedar, and Kirby smelled the smoke from his fireplace. He loved that scent and often thought if one could bottle it, could make it into rearview mirror air fresheners or potpourri, it might be worth a fortune. He approached the creek. Tiny panes of glass-like ice lined the limestone banks and water gurgled down its ice-free center. Kirby noticed the tracks there, fresh tracks in the mud and in the dusting of new snow, made by dozens of paws. The sun had fallen behind the ridge, the shadows long and he had forgotten a flashlight. He stood still. Silence.

"Are you out there my furry friends?" Kirby called. "I'm not that skinner up the road. I'm your buddy. Don't eat me, okay?" He chuckled, and then listened again—nothing. He felt sure they were nearby, and even if out of their sight he knew he was not out of their scent. He imagined them sniffing him and looking around at one another, appraising him. But darkness approached and the snow increased a bit. It would be a white Christmas. Kirby turned back. No sense in stumbling around in the dark woods.

On the way back he thought that perhaps he could incorporate coyotes, or better yet wolves into *Messianic*

Man Returns, the temporary title he wrote under. Maybe as his *Man* resurfaces out of the southern Idaho mountain wilderness where he and his 'disciples' had been cornered and presumably wiped out, he returns like Jesus from the wilderness, alone except for a pack of wolves or coyotes that accompany him just out of sight, protecting him. Kirby was not a writer committed in stone to a pre-drawn outline and he was not sure they could be worked in, but it might be worth a try.

Carefully making his way back up the trail that the deer must have constructed to feast on the maple seedlings that he fruitlessly planted in his yard each year, Kirby stopped, turned and listened, wondering if the coyotes followed. No sound betrayed their presence, but then he hadn't expected any. And what would he have done if he heard leaves rustling nearby... probably sprinted to the kitchen door.

Inside, he brewed a pot of his Swedish Royal Vinter kaffe stash, put two logs on the fire in his study and returned to the manuscript. He felt a late night brewing. Before the first keys clicked, the coyotes began again, heard faintly outside. Kirby smiled and sat a moment listening. Beautiful, and at times their intricate harmonies became comical. What might they be saying? He reached for the remote and clicked off the stereo in the middle of Burl Ives' rendition of 'Frosty,' never one of his favorites. For several hours he slurped coffee and wrote to his outdoor coyote serenade.

Sometime after midnight the crooning ceased and Kirby switched the Christmas music back on. He wrote for another hour and what he had written was good stuff. He slept well for a while.

He dreamt of a time before the success and fame, a time when the kids were little and his love for Tanya was still strong. The rapid-fire dream commingled a procession of Christmases. He and the kids played Hungry, Hungry, Hippo, the world's loudest, clackiest game—a present from his sister-in-law who he would pay back in kind on a Christmas when her kids were old enough. Tanya prepared supper in the kitchen of their three bedroom Lenexa, Kansas, ranch, calling out hilarious comments to her family and to the hippos. The house filled with laughter. The dream included reading 'The Night Before Christmas' and Bill Vaughn's annual newspaper Christmas story to the kids, and other snapshots of Christmases past.

What part of him determined the dreams that would be shown for his REM viewing pleasure had always been a mystery. When he awoke, needing to dispense with the quart of Vinter coffee he had consumed, he remembered his bittersweet Christmas dream. And he recalled those Christmases and those times that could never be recaptured. Kids grew up and moved out, that was normal. But he hadn't changed, Tanya had. She became irritable and less tolerant of his little foibles. She grew jealous of his success and his commitment to writing. It was her fault the marriage had crashed and burned, her fault there were no more such Christmases. Kirby flushed the toilet in the master bath, the room where they had often made love, and returned to bed.

This time sleep eluded him. He lay awake re-plotting his book. Maybe he should make wholesale changes. Maybe his *Man* wouldn't turn out to be a world-class con artist, maybe he *was* the Anti-Christ. Eventually he slept.

Startled, he sat up and waited for his head to clear in the dark bedroom. It was still night but something woke him. The coyotes outside. This was no serenade. It sounded as if a war raged—anger and desperation in their voices. Kirby quickly dressed, and for a moment he wasn't sure why. Downstairs he put on his coat and grabbed a flashlight but stopped near the kitchen door and returned to his study. He opened the bottom right desk drawer and grabbed his father's old .38 police special. He knew what he was about to do was foolish, but he opened the door.

As soon as he stepped outside the caterwauling ceased, except for one voice, weak and strained. The snow had stopped, leaving about two inches, and Kirby tread carefully down the deer trail that led to the creek, the beam from his flashlight bounced ahead. Again he noticed fresh paw tracks when he reached the downward slope. The sound ahead changed from yelping and whining to rapid panting as his beam found the coyote.

It lay on the trail in a small pool of blood, its right front paw clamped by a steel foothold trap. A trickle of blood led up from the creek. Kirby shined his light on the creek's far side where he saw matted snow and the same trickle of blood. The coyote, soaking wet, had dragged itself, the trap and its chain across the creek and now lay in semi-consciousness panting rapidly. Keeping his distance, he examined the leg. It appeared that much of the damage to the leg had come from the coyote or coyotes chewing at it, trying to free it. Nonetheless, it looked bad.

He stuck the .38 in his pants, then approached the animal and placed his foot on its neck to keep it from biting. He bent over and tried to open the trap. The animal offered a half-hearted snarl as he did so. The trap's jaws would not budge. In the nearness, the animal exuded a familiar wet dog scent, a smell absent from his life since Tanya had left him, taking with her their water-loving shepherd-lab mix, Arrow. Kirby thought he heard growling in the woods and he stepped away from the prone animal, stomped his feet and yelled, grabbing for the gun. He stood still and listened. Either the snarling ceased, or he had imagined it in the first place. Kirby swung his light in a circle around him; his gun barrel followed the light. He saw nothing except tracks.

Turning back to the animal, he noted brown-irised yellow eyes that were fixed and glassy, its tongue lolled and it displayed no movement except for the rapid heaving of its chest as it breathed. Standing above it, Kirby noticed it was a male. What should he do? There was no way he was getting the trap off the coyote out here. He considered letting nature take its course, and then after Christmas he'd call the Sheriff on his neighbor. He would show him the carcass. Perhaps it was legal to trap coyotes, but this was *his* land. Or was it possible that this coyote had drug that trap almost a quarter mile from inside Martin's property? And how had he gotten the chain fastener off of the trap's post? It didn't matter. What mattered was what he would do with the animal now? His brain and his intellect made the decision; it was time to let nature handle it and head back to the house, and he did.

At the kitchen door, he felt two dozen eyes staring at him from the woods, and when he swung the flashlight he thought he saw, but couldn't verify, movement just ahead of the light's arc. This was playing out like one of his horror stories. The coyotes would attack him and ride him down and tear him to shreds as he reached for the door handle. Kirby hurried inside and then locked the door, as if coyotes knew how to turn the knob.

Wide awake and in his study, he stirred the fireplace coals but there were not enough to rekindle the fire. He sat at his desk and opened his *Man Returns* story file. Kirby stared at the half full 121st page. He always left his stories in mid-sentence so he would at least be able to start by finishing the sentence that he had begun earlier. That way he would never begin by staring blankly at the screen.

Kirby stared blankly at the screen. He could not pick up his train of thought or even finish the sentence from a few hours ago. Outside dawn approached. Through the window he watched individual trees materialize out of the night's blackness. He found he could not divorce his thoughts of his manuscript with those of the coyote.

Kirby pushed back his chair and rose. He took stairs two at a time up to one of the unused second floor bedrooms, pulled off the spread and the top sheet and returned to the study, again pulling the .38 out of his desk. In the kitchen, he slid a half-gallon carton of orange juice out of the fridge and gulped down nearly a pint straight from the spout—another of the foibles that had irked Tanya. He pulled on a pair of bibs hanging on the coat pegs by the door and then added his Carhartt and boots. A look out the kitchen window convinced him he would not need a flashlight, as the sun was about to crawl over the ridge behind Martin's chicken ranch.

He stepped outside to a clear, cold day. Yesterday's storm had given way to Midwest high pressure cold. With the bedding over his shoulder and the gun in his hand, he found the path and as he walked it dawned on him that the .38 was a revolver. If this were a Kirby horror story, which it might yet become, he had six bullets against at least a dozen coyotes by his reckoning. Up ahead he heard rustling and saw flickers of movement through the trees. He reached to his belt and touched the comfort of the .38.

Kirby approached the prone coyote which had not moved much from the spot he left him. The snow around the animal had been trampled by his pack and their tracks led off west, uphill. The animal still breathed, its panting shallower and more frequent. His eyes followed Kirby's approach, but his head did not move. Before he went to the animal Kirby scanned the hillside above him for signs of his lurking mates. Seeing nothing, he left the .38 in his belt. He placed his foot on the coyote's neck to keep his head motionless and knelt down next to him. The steam from Kirby's breath mingled in the cold air with the coyote's as he lifted its body and slid the bedding underneath. The animal did not resist.

Kirby wrapped the coyote's body in the bedding, laying the trap's chain on top of its chest. He bunched the bedspread around the animal's neck so he could not bend it to bite him, and then carefully picked the coyote up. The coyote voiced a brief yelp at being moved and gave Kirby a rictal snarl. As Kirby returned to the house, he had no doubt that the other coyotes followed. They kept their distance, but made no effort to hide— not a good sign. Coyotes didn't do that. They didn't "pack" like wolves and they kept hidden. Kirby wondered if maybe he held the mate of one of them, and that at some point they would cut him off and try to free him, try to keep him from being skinned by the human. The gun in his belt did him no good as long as he held the coyote.

"Get away," he shouted. The coyote in his arms twitched and whined and was silent. Unexpectedly, Brady Kirby felt tears rolling down his cheeks. "I'm trying to help him, for God's sake," he said, this time more quietly and his voice broke as he spoke. The coyotes continued to pace him at the top of the rise, eighty feet away. He stopped. They stopped.

Kirby hurried on and now he could see the clearing and the slate roof of his house. His quickened pace bounced the animal in his arms and it groaned with each step so Kirby slowed. If the coyotes wanted to attack him they could at any time and hurrying wouldn't change that. Tears were replaced by determination. If they got any closer, he would drop the damn animal, rely on the quick draw he practiced incessantly as a child, and plug a few before they rode him down in a flurry of teeth, claws and jaws. He discovered he was grinding his teeth and so he chewed the side of his tongue instead.

The coyotes accompanied him to the clearing but remained at the edge of the woods in plain sight. They watched him approach the kitchen door. They looked ready to spring. Kirby shifted his load and grasped the knob. He swung open the door and stepped inside, looking over his shoulder. The coyotes still stood at the tree-line, their heads down and teeth barred like dogs ready for a fight. He took the animal into his study and laid it by the fireplace, leaving it covered. The coyote's eyes were closed; it shivered, its breathing shallow. The musty smell of his old wet dog, Arrow, a distant memory until today, once again wafted up as he built a fire. When the fire began to crackle and pop, the coyote's eyes snapped open and in them he saw an abject fear, perhaps of the flames. Kirby moved him away, across to the far side of the room by his bookshelves near his desk. The animal's eyes closed.

Kirby went to his desk, fired up his PC and searched for traps. He found a Wildlife and Parks web site with a 4-H study guide explaining different traps and their operation. His eyes bounced between the text and the coyote, which did not move except for his heaving chest. Kirby found the trap for which he was looking. He needed to step on the two wings simultaneously to pop it open.

He returned to the animal and pulled away the spread. Kirby saw that he would need to twist the coyote's injured leg some to line up the trap properly. Again he placed his foot on its neck, bent over and as gently as possible moved the leg. The coyote yelped and struggled and tried to free his head for a few moments and then lay back again breathing hard. The leg was in an awkward position that must have been painful and Kirby needed both feet free to open the trap. He removed his foot from the coyote's throat, repositioned the trap and quickly stepped with both feet on the wings. Simultaneously, the trap sprung open and the coyote bit him on the calf. Its bite came from pain and instinct, but had little strength behind it. Nonetheless, it stung and Kirby jumped back and felt for the gun under his bibs.

The animal lay back on his side, his ankle now free of the trap, but he was unable to rise. Kirby limped out of the study, sliding the French doors shut. In the kitchen he reached above the sink for the first aid shoebox. Outside he saw the coyotes were still at the edge of the woods and one sat on haunches a half-dozen paces into the yard, its cold yellow eyes watching the house. He set the box on the table and pulled up his pant leg. There were no puncture marks penetrating his skin, but a nasty abrasion ran along the shin where a tooth that failed to penetrate duck bib and denim scraped not quite harmlessly along the shinbone. Kirby squirted a slick of Neosporin and slapped two band aids horizontally, one above the other, on his hairy leg.

He grabbed the first aid box and a half-full quart of peroxide from the refrigerator then returned to the study. The animal had not moved, but his eyes opened as the doors slid apart. Kirby approached.

"It's okay fella," he said softly. "I'm not going to hurt you." Kirby knew that wasn't wholly true as the peroxide would sting. And he didn't know if anything he did would help. The animal seemed pretty far gone. As he knelt, the coyote's eyes followed him, its tongue hung loosely out of its mouth, lying on the bedspread. Kirby twisted off the peroxide cap and carefully rested his knee on the coyote's neck.

"Now this may sting a little," he said as if he was treating Ben or Katie's small-child skinned knee. He poured it on the torn flesh. The animal yelped and jerked twice, feet kicking and then was still, whining like Arrow used to do when he wanted out. Once the foaming subsided, he dabbed the peroxide and blood with a corner of the top sheet.

"Take it easy now, the worst is over." His voice wavered; again he felt himself close to tears. The animal's soft whine continued. These feelings of compassion and empathy had long been absent in his solitary life of writing and traveling the country making public appearances. He knew how to write of those feelings, but no longer lived with them. Using a light touch he dabbed on Neosporin and lifted the leg to wrap the bandage. The coyote's head twitched momentarily. When he had fastened the bandage, Kirby laid the leg back down and went to his desk. In the Miami County directory he found the number of Osawatomie's sole veterinarian. After three rings, he got a happy holidays message and a number to call for emergencies. Would a vet consider this an emergency? He dialed the number and got another voice mail. Kirby left a message and a number.

For several hours he sat and wrote his manuscript and watched the coyote, mostly the latter. The animal's breathing seemed to evolve from panting to rasping. Kirby rose and returned to the kitchen, not bothering to slide the study doors closed. In the kitchen he rifled through drawers. Out the window in bright sunlight, made even brighter by the reflective brilliance of new snow, the coyotes had retreated into the woods but were still visible. A lone coyote—the same one?—rested on haunches at the edge of the trees. Kirby continued his search through the drawers. Tanya had taken with her most of the accoutrements of their lives as spousal meal preparers, but he found what he was looking for, an old turkey baster. He filled a large plastic cup with cool water, stuck the tip in and squeezed the bulb. It still worked, filling with water.

Back in the study he knelt over the coyote, held the baster inches over his mouth and squeezed a few drops. The animal's eyes sprang open and its tongue moved for the first time in an hour. Kirby squeezed again, and then some more. The animal lapped it up.

He squirted the whole glass, much of it ran off into the bedspread but the animal lapped a good deal of it and showed signs of the struggle to live. He refilled the glass and squeezed until the animal no longer tried to drink, then returned to his desk and observed. Kirby thought its breathing sounded better but it might be wishful thinking.

A little later he fixed a sandwich and opened a bag of Fritos, his Christmas Eve supper. The coyote slept, but its breathing still was rapid and rough. Kirby continued to write distractedly and he switched on Sirius classic Christmas music at very low volume. He didn't know how the coyote would react to Dean Martin, Emmy Lou Harris and the others. It didn't react. It just lay there.

"So tell me, is that your gang out there?" Kirby smiled and the coyote opened his eyes at his voice, or at least the eye that faced the room's beamed ceiling. "And what about the one that waits in the yard, is she female, your mate maybe?" The coyote did not move and closed its eyes.

"What's the matter, cat got your tongue?" Kirby leaned back in his chair chuckling.

The sun was setting and the coyote seemed no better or worse. The vet never called. Kirby walked to the kitchen and turned on the back porch light. The single coyote in the yard jumped to its feet preparing to flee to the woods, then found Kirby in the window and stared at him as it curled up again in the backyard snow. Kirby could not see if the others were in the woods, but he knew they were. He spotted an area in the yard where the snow was trampled, twenty feet long. This animal must have been pacing.

Back in the study, a proofread found today's writing stunted and lifeless and he eventually just watched his cursor flash in mid-sentence until the screen saver kicked in. And then he watched the coyote breathe and the screen saver fish swim around in their tropical desk monitor fishbowl. The Christmas music played on. He fell asleep.

He awoke to the howl of coyotes just outside his window and the renewed whining of his canine guest, who still lay on the bedding. A small patch of blood had seeped through the bandages. He would change them in the morning if the animal was still alive. Kirby's neck was stiff from sleeping in his desk chair and from an old college rugby injury, compliments of the Denver Barbarians. He rubbed it as he went to the kitchen and flicked the porch light on and off several times. The noise outside ceased, though he could still hear dog-like whining coming from the study. He drew another glass of water; this time he dissolved two aspirin in it, and took the glass and the baster into the study, where once again the coyote drank it up. Kirby slid the doors shut and went to bed.

He lay awake for a while and his mind rambled. It cycled through memories of his young family when Tanya was the one with the steady paychecks and the fledgling writer stayed home with the kids, nursing their cuts and bruises, colds and the flu. He remembered hurrying Katie to the Olathe medical center when her arm was so badly broken skating on the driveway. Maybe he should have taken the coyote to a vet clinic in the city.

For a moment he even considering praying for the animal, though he could not remember one sincere prayer offered in his adult life. God and Jesus were pushed on him by his parents, and following his confirmation he tapered off church attendance as much as his parents would allow. As an adult he used to attend the occasional Easter or Christmas service with Tanya and the kids out of obligation and familial cohesion.

God was a myth to comfort the weak who couldn't handle their own problems; the Bible a load of fairy tales, full of retribution and cheesy miracles. He was surprised it had remained on the bestseller list so long. Of course so did the crap Dan Brown churned out. Any

39

prayer offered would be disingenuous at best. The animal's life wasn't in God's hands, but his. And he had done the best he could. Kirby prepared himself to find a carcass on his hardwood floor in the morning.

He thought about the animal downstairs and about his pack outside. And Kirby realized that he had no pack, that he had no one really. He had an editor, and a publisher and an agent. He had fans wherever he went. He had women of all ages that wanted him even though Tanya didn't. He had success. But he didn't have what that coyote had, a pack that loved him and looked out for him as a reflection of that love. Sure the kids loved him, but he felt that maybe it was the obligatory love that a child feels for a parent. Did they even like him? These long repressed thoughts flowed up from his gut, bashing him like waves bash against a rocky shore, one after another. He couldn't stop the flow. They kept coming, but fatigue held sway and he dozed off.

Once again he awoke to the wild howling of angry animals. Worse, they seemed to be inside the house. Thumps and crashes and banging from below confirmed. He sprang from his bed, pulled on some sweat pants and reached into the closet for his boyhood Ken Boyer model Louisville Slugger baseball bat. The gun, unfortunately, had been returned to the drawer downstairs. With the bat in his right hand, he stepped out into the hall. The crashing below, coupled with short, choppy coyote yipping, continued.

He crept down the stairs. Early morning light streaked into the family room windows leaving it in deep shadows, but there seemed to be no disturbance here. The noise came from the kitchen and the study and from outside. He flipped on the lights at the bottom of the stairs and he could see shards of glass on the kitchen floor. Something threw itself against the still closed French doors of the study to his left, and, after a few moments, again. This time one of the doors partially jumped off its overhead track. A third thud flopped the door down into the foyer. A coyote—his coyote— skittered across it and into the family room where it collided with an end table sending a lamp crashing to the floor, plunging that portion of the room into darkness.

Wailing and crashing from the kitchen increased and Kirby's coyote leaped that way. Once in the kitchen it slid across the terrazzo and the shards of broken glass, smashing itself into the kitchen table which sent Kirby's coffee mug flying. Kirby warily followed as his coyote was now out of sight in the far corner of the kitchen. When he reached the kitchen archway he found the glass had been shattered out of the mullioned window panes at the top of the back door. There were at least several animals banging themselves against the door from outside. Kirby's Coyote threw himself against the inside of the door. Kirby saw the bloodstained bandage still on his leg. The red smear had not increased much. He knew those outside and his coyote inside had each other's scent, which ramped up their ferocity.

Without thinking of what might be prudent, or even sane, he hurried to the door and swung it inward. His coyote sprang outside. No animals hurled themselves in at him. They all chased after Kirby's coyote, dancing and spinning in the yard before darting away into the woods. One coyote, the one who had waited in his yard, Kirby thought, stopped at the edge of the woods, turned back and looked at him. Whenever Brady Kirby told this story, afterward, he swore that the coyote nodded to him, but the sun had not fully risen and it might have been his imagination.

Kirby shut the door and dropped into a chair next to his catawampus kitchen table, cold Christmas air blowing in through the broken window. He noticed that he had cut both feet on the glass and there was no small amount of blood on the floor. Was it all his, he wondered? The open first aid box still lay there on the kitchen counter and he leaned over and grabbed it. He doctored on one foot and then the other. There was a gouge in the arch of his left foot that he supposed ought to have stitches—maybe tomorrow after Christmas.

Cleaned and bandaged, with gauze wrapped all the way around his left foot, he stood and looked out the window over the sink. No sign of the coyotes. He pulled a roll of duct tape out of the utility drawer and carefully limped over to the back door where he taped his bibs over the broken window—ah, wonderful duct tape. In the pantry he retrieved the broom and dust pan and swept up the broken glass. Always wise to do barefooted so that your feet will inform you if you missed anything, Kirby thought with a chuckle. Then he put on a pot of coffee.

The kitchen clock read 6:55. While he waited for the coffee, which his shaking hands and stinging feet needed badly, he wondered how his coyote could have made such a miraculous recovery. Not miraculous, miraculous required a belief that someone was pulling the strings, God or Jesus or Buddha or whoever. He settled on the term 'such a speedy recovery.' But how did he do it? The coyote seemed in such bad shape last night and fifteen minutes ago he was knocking down doors. "Tis a puzzlement," he said out loud, one of his lines from his high school production of *The King and I.* The coffee was ready. He poured himself a cup and hobbled to his study. He stepped over the door that was laid out like a ship's gang plank and into the room.

It was trashed. His first thought was the computer. He hadn't shut it off or saved what he had written before he fell asleep last night. But the computer and his desk seemed okay, although his chair had been rolled across the room and slammed into a floor lamp now pinned against the wall.

Books were everywhere. Several shelves had collapsed and would need repair. He dropped to his knees and began to stack books on the floor near the damaged and depleted shelves. Kirby crawled around the room bare-chested, with bare bandaged feet, retrieving books; his Faulkner first editions, his Keats and Yeats and Hardy from college.

When he had accomplished as much as he could on his knees, Kirby crawled over to his desk and took a sip of coffee. He noticed that his shakes had stopped and he stepped gingerly back into the kitchen to grab the coffee pot. The kitchen clock showed that it was nearly 8:00 a.m.

Kirby returned to his desk, set the coffee pot down on his blotter and wiggled the mouse. The cursor still blinked on last night's unfinished sentence. He watched the cursor flash on his *Messianic Man Returns* Word file. A cold draft from the kitchen numbed the pain in his feet as the cursor's tiny hypnotic blinking and its accomplice, the fatigue of stress, caused him to drift off.

Again he dreamt. He ran with the coyotes. He was one of them, a part of the pack. They all gathered at the hilltop. Kirby stood next to the coyote that paced his backyard and they all howled at the moon, his voice harmonizing with his friends and family.

He snapped awake, his neck sore as hell. The clock on his monitor showed he had only been asleep for twenty minutes. Brady Kirby gulped the remainder of lukewarm coffee from his cup and stood, careful to keep his weight on his uninjured heels. He shook his wrists and rubbed his sore neck, then picked up his cell phone and dialed the number he had almost forgotten.

"Hello, Tanya?"

Embers

Mark Meriwether woke with a start. Where was he? What strange place was this? Gradually it came to him—his childhood bedroom in St. Paul, Kansas. He'd slept in this tiny single bed until he fled his parents' house for Kansas University twenty-four years ago. Outside his second-floor window the snow still swirled in the ever-present Kansas wind. *Christmas morning.* But what about last night—had it been a dream? He reflected on that question as he slid his feet out of bed and planted them on his great-grandmother's hand-braided rug.

He didn't want to think about last night. He wanted to delete the drive home from his cranial inbox.

When he was a kid, Mark used the braided rings of the rug below him as an oval race track for Matchbox cars. He'd roll dice and move each car the requisite car lengths. He hid his dice in a pair of sneakers in his closet. His father would not abide dice in the house.

Mark's brain kept coming back to the trip home last night. Had it really happened?

***

Late afternoon on Christmas Eve Mark drove south on US 59 from Lawrence. He rode alone. Keri had the kids for Christmas this year. He'd had them for Thanksgiving. Big fat snowflakes floated and swirled in the moderate north wind. Eastern Kansas would have a rare white Christmas as four to six inches were forecast by morning.

He thought about the white Christmases he'd pined for as a kid. But in that perfect wheelhouse of years for a boy and snow, he'd missed them all—unless one counted his ninth year when three-inches fell on December twenty-first, and still lingered in lonely shady patches on Christmas morning. He didn't count it.

There had been several snowy holidays since he'd become an adult. With adulthood, however, he'd learned what a damned hassle snow could be. But there was that one year when his kids were young and he and Keri were still a family. They'd all frolicked in snowball fights, loaded up the SUV, and tobogganed down the short but thrillingly steep hill in North Lawrence on the levee by the Kaw River.

Jason and Jenny were in high school now, and with every passing year their ferocious fires of childhood dimmed, dwindling to the eventual embers of memory. Mark shook off those thoughts and tuned to 102.1 radio, nearby Kansas City's all-Christmas music channel. He cranked up the volume as Elvis placed his stamp on the old Crosby standard, "White Christmas." Mark's father once had an uncanny knack for Elvis's voice, style, and inflection. He even accomplished the physical gyrations. Frank Meriwether could have made a living as an Elvis impersonator had he not placed his feet on the path to Baptist ministry. Those years, like childhood, were his own embers of memory, brightening briefly at recall.

Mark sang along with Elvis, thinking of his dad.

His dad.

He loved his dad, but sometimes he hated him—so absorbed with Christ and his Bible that he failed to see anything else. So judgmental for someone whose book tells him to judge not lest he be judged. In college Mark became friends with two other preachers' sons in his fraternity. Mark discovered the love-hate thing with your dad was not uncommon for a preacher's son, and neither was such a son coming out of adolescence an atheist.

Frank Meriwether had never been satisfied with anything his only son accomplished, and never would be. So, Mark had quit trying to please his father. He'd become very successful at not pleasing him. That's why he dreaded his twice annual trip to St. Paul on Thanksgiving and again on Christmas.

His sister Sarah had told him he was too hard on Dad, that he created opportunities to argue. Arguments then escalated, which according to Sarah spoiled family holidays. Sarah was wrong. Dad had always been the aggressor.

***

Traffic had been rush-hour slow southbound on the drive to Ottawa, but after he crossed underneath Interstate 35 the traffic on US 59 evaporated. The good news—less traffic. The bad news—more snow on the highway and no well-worn tracks to follow. Still, a plow had hit the southbound lanes recently, and it wasn't bad.

The marker read *Garnett 16* and then another sixty miles from there to St. Paul. The dash clock showed a quarter after four. It would be dark soon, only four days after Winter Solstice, the shortest day of the year. Pagans celebrated Solstice with decorated trees, wreaths, holly, and gift giving. At some point around a thousand years ago these pagan Solstice celebrations had been tied to the birth of Jesus. Mark's dad refused to listen when he tried to argue that Christmas was more pagan than Christian. And Mark was sure they would find something similar to fight about during the next seventy-two hours.

The road went through downtown Garnett, which bustled with last-minute holiday hunters and gatherers. Mark remembered one summer long ago Dad had taken him and Mom and his younger sister Sarah to the Grand Prix auto races at Lake Garnett. He couldn't have been more than ten, and his and Dad's relationship had not yet soured. Two days of races, all kinds of cars, from little sports cars to roaring Ferraris, Lotuses, and Corvettes. They had picnicked, laughed often, and even stayed in a motel with a pool.

Just south of Garnett, US 169 intersected with 59 Highway. Both would get him to St. Paul, 59 the shorter route, 169 the better, more traveled highway. After a moment's consideration, Mark thought of a Robert Frost poem from a KU English class where *two roads diverged and I, took the one less traveled by.*

Within ten miles, and well before he reached Moran, Mark wished he'd taken 169. Though the highway here had been treated earlier in the afternoon, the snow had overwhelmed the salt treatment. Its pavement needed a plow. Mark slowed a bit. After all, he was in no hurry to get there. He'd told Mom not to plan on him for dinner, and the less time he spent around his holier than thou father the better.

With Moran in his rearview mirror the radio station began to cut out. He searched for another, one hand on the wheel and one hand tapping the search button, his eyes ping-ponging between the digital numbers and the roadway. He found a Joplin, Missouri, station playing Christmas music. Atheist or not, Mark loved Christmas music.

He listened to Vince Gill and Gill's daughter, Jenny, singing "Let There Be Peace on Earth" as he neared the small town of Erie, struggling to exist in the twenty-first century when so many similar Kansas towns trickled away into memory. His hometown, St. Paul, was in a similar plight, and his father had always been an anomaly—a Baptist preacher in a small Catholic town.

The lifeblood of Prairie Baptist Church had been farming families in the rural areas outside of town. But corporate farms and the vagaries of weather and crop prices gradually winked them out of existence. Mark knew his dad's church was in trouble. He wondered if Frank Meriwether, at his age, could start over somewhere else.

Vince and Jenny Gill finished their duet. Mark thought of his own Jenny. She would be off to college in a year. Mark's Jenny had picked up the love of carols from him. She had a beautiful singing voice and had sat-in with the Prairie Baptist choir on Christmas Eve a time or two when she was in her early teens—more memory embers.

Mark neared Erie, a town of just over a thousand people in the last census, though surely it had shrunk since. Headlights and flashers cut through the darkness and the blowing snow in the northbound lane opposite him. Mark slowed.

As his SUV crept past, he made out an older model Chevy with its trunk open. An elderly couple stood at the trunk. The woman held a flashlight as the man pulled out a "donut" spare tire. They both were underdressed for such a task. Mark noticed a scissor jack in the accumulated snow at the man's feet. After passing them he nursed the SUV back up to snowy highway speed. That sucks. Thank god it wasn't me, Mark thought.

As the Chevy's taillights and flashers disappeared from his rearview mirror, the logical side of Mark's brain commenced a quick but spirited debate with his emotional side. "Shit," Mark said aloud at the debate's conclusion.

He pulled a U-turn at the Erie exit and headed back north. His logical side reminded him he hadn't brought any gloves. "Shit," Mark said again.

He pulled off on the narrow shoulder leaving his headlights shining on the Chevy, and flicked on his flashers.

***

"Breakfast in fifteen minutes, Mark. Are you up?" His mom called from downstairs.

"Sort of," he responded. "I'm awake, anyway."

"Dad wants you to bring in some firewood before breakfast. Can you get dressed and do that, please?"

"It's snowing out." Did he sound like he was whining?

"Yes, I know. Isn't it lovely?"

"Can't it wait until after breakfast?"

There was a pause before Mark's mother answered. "That's a question best posed to your father."

"Shit," Mark muttered to himself—a common word made more common by this trip. He dressed hurriedly. His boots were still wet from last night. He should have left them near the fireplace. Downstairs he grabbed his coat from the closet and his old Kansas City Chiefs stocking cap from the top shelf. On the back porch he instinctively reached into his coat pocket for his gloves before he remembered they were at home.

Inside one pocket was a slip of paper, folded once. One side had jagged edges, as if it had been torn from a small journal. He unfolded the sheet.

***

The old man, on both knees by the driver's side rear wheel, watched him approach. The woman came to meet Mark.

"Thank God, you stopped. We have a flat and my husband can't get the jack to work." She took Mark's arm and nearly dragged him to where her husband kneeled as if he were praying to the god of scissor jacks. Mark dropped down next to him.

"Show me what's wrong," Mark asked.

The old man pointed. His face, wet from melting snowflakes, glistened in the glare of Mark's car headlights. The light blazed on the ridges of the man's wrinkles and accented their deep dark valleys. He must have been at least eighty. The jack was fully extended, yet it had only raised the springs a bit, leaving the tire unmoved.

"Here's your problem," Mark said. "You've got the jack in the wrong place. Let's look in front of the wheel."

Mark and the man slid over to the front side and Mark noticed the man had no gloves either. His hands formed claws and he kept blowing on them. "Shine your

49

flashlight right here," Mark said to the woman. "Ah, yeah, here's where we need to put the jack. We'll need to crank it way down in order to slide it in."

The man slid over and began turning the tire tool counter-clockwise, but his hands wouldn't cooperate.

"Here, let me do it." Mark quickly lowered the jack, though his cold hands complained. It wouldn't be long before they were as clawed as the old man's. He told the man to stand up and hand him the spare when he asked for it.

Mark made quick work of removing the flat. As he worked, they introduced themselves as Matthew and Mary. When Mark asked where they were headed, they merely said they still had a long way to go that night. "Well, take it nice and slow on this donut," Mark had said.

When Mark was ready, Matthew's claw-hands rolled the little tire to him through the thickening snow. Five minutes later Mark was loading their trunk with the jack, tool, and offending tire.

He turned to the couple. "You're ready to go."

Matthew had his wallet out. He fumbled for money.

"Oh, no. I won't accept anything," Mark said. "Call it a Christmas present."

"Then you must accept our thanks," she said, and hugged him for a length of time that made Mark begin to feel uncomfortable. She released him from her bear hug, though she still held tightly onto his forearms. "God bless you, young man." Mark shook mutually frozen hands with Matthew and he returned to his car. When he slid into the seat the first thing he did was crank the heat up to high. When he looked up, the Chevy was already gone.

"Wow, that was quick."

Mark looked around to make sure no cars were coming. As he pulled forward to initiate another U-turn he stopped. His headlights showed his footprints to and from the departed Chevy. The snow around where the flat had been changed was greatly disturbed. There were no other footprints, nor were there any tire tracks.

Mark got out of the car and walked forward. Nothing. Only his footprints there and back, around the tire, and where the trunk must have been. There was no hint of the trail the donut tire made when Matthew rolled it to him, No tire tracks at all.

He returned to his car and sat in its warmth for a long time, flashers flashing, puzzling what had taken place. At least three radio carols came and went.

Mark didn't tell his parents or his sister and her family what had happened on the way to St. Paul. His mom would think he'd suffered a brain aneurism. His dad would think he was on drugs, which would have been a possibility two decades ago.

***

On the back porch, a strong wind blew stinging snow pellets in his face. He wanted to get back inside as quickly as possible. He looked down at the paper. In a shaky longhand was written: *God bless you, Mark Meriwether. Matthew 25: 35-40.*

While Mark collected his first armload of firewood, he thought back. He knew his pockets were empty when he left Lawrence. The lady named Mary might have stuck it there when she hugged him. More likely his father went to the closet and stuck the note in his pocket after he had gone to bed—a sneaky way to remind him that he should come back into the fold. Yeah, that was it. Because Mark had never told Mary his last name. He couldn't remember the passage, not unusual since he'd divorced the Bible from his life more than two decades ago.

Years earlier his dad had tried to let Mark's nonbelieving go. But he just couldn't. Mark supposed for Frank Meriwether it was a big deal. It all made sense. Dad wanted to save his son from an eternity in hell. That's what Dad believed. He was welcome to it, just as Mark should be welcome not to believe.

After breakfast Mark went upstairs to his room. He opened his long untouched Bible and flipped to Matthew 25:

[35] For I was hungry and you gave me something to eat, I was thirsty and you gave me something to drink, I was a stranger and you invited me in,[36] I needed clothes and you clothed me, I was sick and you looked after me, I was in prison and you came to visit me.'

[37] "Then the righteous will answer him, 'Lord, when did we see you hungry and feed you, or thirsty and give you something to drink?[38] When did we see you a stranger and invite you in, or needing clothes and clothe you? [39] When did we see you sick or in prison and go to visit you?'

[40] "The King will reply, 'Truly I tell you, whatever you did for one of the least of these brothers and sisters of mine, you did for me.'

He reread the passage.

"Mark, honey, come down and be sociable. We're going to open presents soon."

"Coming, Mom." Mark changed into his red dress shirt, but decided to forgo the Santa tie that always irked his dad. He slipped the note into his shirt pocket.

***

On Christmas night, after a meal of spiral-sliced ham and all the trimmings, they sat around the fireplace. On the stereo, Randy Travis crooned about an old-fashioned Christmas. It had been a good day. No fights with Dad. Sarah's young and surprisingly well-behaved kids were in bed and she had opened a bottle of Merlot. Dad, who didn't drink, had a cup of coffee on the end table. Mark sat on the couch with Mom and Sarah's husband, Dave. Mark stared into the fire, following the flame's flicker. As he watched the fiery dance he realized a part of him had known from the moment he read the note that it wasn't his father's handwriting.

"You've been quiet all day," Sarah said.

No one answered. Mark turned away from the fire to see Sarah looking directly at him.

"Who, me?"

"Yes, Mark. Is there something wrong?" his mom asked

"Nope. Everything's fine. Just thinking about something."

"Uh oh, batten down the hatches, Mark's been thinking," Sarah said. The grin on her face told Mark she was teasing. But he also saw the look behind the grin, the one that said, please don't set off Dad.

A loud pop brought Mark's attention back to the fire. The flames steeled him to do what he wasn't sure he wanted to do.

After a moment of silence, everyone thinking their own thoughts, Mark pulled the note from his pocket and said, "Hey, everyone, I want to tell you a story, a true story."

Naming Christmas

Frazzled. He thought that might be a fitting name, or maybe Glum, but hopefully not Marriage Shattering; no they would be okay somehow. Every year since their engagement in 1989, Marvin and Tina Larson had named their Christmases. Like the Snow Christmas, which fell in ninety-three when Kansas City not only had a rare white Christmas, but experienced three days of layered snow totaling almost a foot, ending the morning of the twenty-fourth. The Bonus Christmas arrived five years later when he sold three houses in December. He remembered feeling like the reformed Scrooge felt waking up that glorious Christmas morning, and like Scrooge, Marvin went nuts buying lavish gifts for Tina, the kids and his extended family.

Most of the other realtors had left for the weekend as he sat at his office desk five days before Christmas. Gazing out at the barren trees along Indian Creek, barren except for the oaks that refused to release their brown, dead leaves, Marvin unfocused from the nightmare that was real estate in the latter half of 2007. He allowed his mind to wander. He recalled their First Christmas when the relationship was so new and fresh and alive. He and Tina were engaged and slept together regularly but kept two separate places. They had decorated a tree at Tina's place, and spent that part of the Christmas holidays not mingling with local friends and relatives at Tina's. Tina had covered her Overland Park apartment with Christmassy knick-knacks. Marvin shopped with her and bought a tree ornament from Hallmark signifying their First Christmas. In some ways the gesture, and the feeling behind it and the promise of the future that little Frosty Friend represented, lent that ornament more significance for them than her engagement ring. They married in January and soon after Tina became pregnant with Trevor, who was born in October. He and Tina dubbed that 1990 holiday Baby's Christmas and bought another ornament.

Marvin secretly began creating alternate names for their Christmases in 1994, which officially became the six-month old infant Brett's Christmas. But for Marvin, Brett's Christmas would forever secretly be the Hot Sex Christmas. Tina had been unable or unwilling to make love since her caesarian-section in July. She had taken the fall semester off from teaching high school history to mother Brett and four-year-old Trevor, so there had been opportunities that fall to make love day and night due to his flexible schedule. But Tina pushed away his advances to the point he had stopped making them. On December sixth—he remembered the exact date—after decorating the tree, including a new ornament for Brett's first Christmas, and after putting the two boys to bed, Tina jumped Marvin on the living room couch and they made love for the first time since May. Marvin and Tina mated like rabbits all through New Years day. For three weeks, whenever both boys slept at the same time, the two made love fervently, leisurely, emphatically, in every nook and cranny of their tiny post-war ranch. So, though Tina referred to that year as Brett's Christmas, Marvin always smiled knowingly, remembering it by another name.

Similarly, the Twins Christmas of 1999, the year Rachael and Francis were born in September, became his Cranky Christmas. Tina had again taken a leave of absence from teaching that fall, affecting their pocket book. And neither had any idea of the added struggles that twins would present in every conceivable way, and in some respects that were previously inconceivable. One night just before Christmas the two boys had finally collapsed on their bunks from sugar and gift-greed induced highs. They slept like angels after acting like devils. The infant twins slept as well, providing a rare moment of restful quiet. Marvin and Tina had been lying in bed fully clothed in their three-year-old suburban split level, the sounds of Vince Gill carols wafting up through the heater vents from the stereo one floor below. The scent of gingerbread cookies baked hours ago still lingered. Tina had whispered, with humor he thought at the time, that God never intended a woman to nurse two infants, and he mirthfully responded, "God gave you two breasts didn't he?" Tina lurched to a sitting position, lighting bolts shot from her eyes, striking him one after another, shrinking and sizzling him like bacon, indicating that perhaps she had misconstrued his sophisticated attempt at humor. Yes, the Twins Christmas would always be his sleep-deprived, walking-on-eggs "Cranky" one.

Now he sat hunched over his desk. The paperwork spread around its deep cherry surface included not one sniff of a homebuyer or commercial lease. But the arrogance of his purchase of Citigroup stock on margin last spring stood in the forefront of his current dilemma. The real estate market had boomed for several years in south KC and he took those profits for granted. Marvin's Brother Ed and his friend Mark made a killing buying bank stock on margin during the boom and hooked him up with their broker. It seemed such a sure thing. Investments tripled in less than a year. He hadn't bothered Tina with the margin buy details and she signed the paper work on the second mortgage with only some cursory questions. She trusted him.

But the bottom fell out of the mortgage industry taking banks like Citigroup that were investors in sub-prime mortgages down with it. Now a margin call loomed on his investment account. Marvin stared out the window at the skeletonized trees. Behind the patch of woods, traffic passed along 103rd street. People hurrying home for the weekend or stopping for last minute gifts, were oblivious of the foolish man who watched them from behind stark trees that stood between them like the bars of a cell. Marvin would need to cash the mutual fund investments they had been saving for college since Trevor was born to cover the margin call, either that or they would foreclose on the house, and even then he would be stuck with margin debt on near worthless stock. How could he tell Tina?

He looked up at the clock on the far wall, the clock with golf clubs for hands and the little orbiting white ball on the tip of the second hand, the clock that Francis and Rachael had given him last Christmas. Ten past five already—too late to liquidate the mutual funds. He would have to take care of it first thing Monday morning, on Christmas Eve. Damn, how could he have been so stupid? Greed, that's how. Would this end up being his Stupid Greed Christmas? Marvin removed his glasses and rubbed the bridge of his nose and his tired eyes. Stress seemed to go after his eyes first. He held the lenses up to his mouth. He puffed, coating them with moistened air and wiped them with a Kleenex from the fancy wood dispenser he had received as a gift from someone sometime. He put the glasses back on. Bare trees and passing cars leaped out at him with startling clarity. People never seem to notice how dirty eyeglasses become when it happens incrementally, almost like gradually losing your eyesight.

The driver and pitching wedge met up near the bottom of his golf clock—almost half past five. Something Tina wanted him to pick up on the way home escaped him. It danced around in his brain avoiding attempts at capture. What was it? Something important, but the things floating around in his head had him frazzled—there was that word again. At best, this would be his Frazzled Christmas, and he didn't want to think about the worst. He picked up his cumbersome black office phone, a dinosaur from the eighties, pressed nine for an outside line and dialed home. Francis answered.

"Did you get the tree yet, dad? Didyuh?"

The tree. That's what he'd forgotten, and he suspected he knew why. Each year Marvin brought the Larson family tree home the first week of December, and a fancy ceremonial tree-trimming, complete with Christmas music and homemade cookies, commenced that weekend. Now, five days left and still no tree. Some days he simply hadn't had time and some days he forgot. He wondered what Freud would say about his failure. The kids had gone from teasing, to badgering, and still he had neglected it. Last night in bed, Tina asked what was bothering him and he had lied, telling her everything was fine, and then he rolled over facing the wall.

"Well, don't forget the tree tomorrow, dear. We're decorating it on Saturday. I love you, g'night." She spooned up to him, resting her hand on his thigh.

He had mumbled his "love you too, goodnight" and pretended to fall right to sleep, but sleep didn't come for some time. None of his old get-to-sleep tricks had worked, not even playing *Do Wah Diddy* over and over inside his head—his version of counting sheep. Her hand resting on his leg hadn't helped either. It seemed more a symbol of accusation than affection. At some point he had slept, but Marvin woke this morning feeling as if he had been awake all night.

Marvin promised Francis that he would be home soon with the tree and hung up. He pulled on his tan, threadbare London Fog overcoat and turned up the collar. The temperatures had plummeted overnight. He loved the overcoat, bought it the winter of his senior year at KU on discount at Weavers with money he had scrapped together working as a stock/delivery boy. Three years ago Tina gave him a new overcoat for the Toothless Christmas—the one both Twins lost teeth on the 23rd and cried, inconsolable the next morning when the tooth fairy failed to show. Marvin and Tina's hurried and harried explanation that Santa would be subbing for the tooth fairy that night hadn't washed for the

Twins who believed they had been cheated by the fairy. Marvin still wore his old coat while the new one Tina had given him remained, hanging fresh and spotless in the hall closet. Tina had been miffed at first, but deep down she understood that this was a "man thing" that she would never fully understand.

At the door, Marvin started to switch off his office light and for the dozenth time remembered the lights had been placed on motion sensors in one of his firm's "green" pushes last summer. He walked to the rear office entrance. Everyone else had already left. His busy Nichols branch office had seemed a ghost town since early November. Marvin didn't ask if some of the realtors were gone for good. If it was true, he just didn't want to know.

The dry rattling sound of leaves chattering across the parking lot accompanied the whoosh of traffic on nearby Metcalf Avenue as he hurried to his Buick, head bowed against the north wind. It was already almost dark. Marvin turned north, and almost immediately hit the red light at 99th Street. Traffic lights peppered Metcalf for the two plus miles up to the Lions Club tree lot: eleven he thought, and the lights were sequenced by some satanic traffic engineer; they triggered according to Marvin's mood. On a good day, they remained green indefinitely, and on a day like today, he knew they would tantalize him, glowing green until the last moment before stopping the Buick in its tracks.

Marvin tried out methods of breaking the financial news to Tina as he and the cars unlucky enough to accompany him north sat through Satan's version of Christmas lights—red, green, red, red, red. He ruled out a humorous approach. There was nothing funny about losing three to five years' tuition and books for the kids. He also thought about timing. Should he spoil Christmas or New Years? Did his thoughts on timing have anything to do with him being plain chicken to tell Tina?

At 75th Street Marvin pulled into the Osco parking lot and drove around behind the store. The small number of trees remaining startled him as he parked next to a string of white lights swaying in the brisk wind. When Marvin climbed out of the Buick, Aaron Ballinger opened the door of the tiny hut that looked like a fancy outhouse and hurried over to meet him.

"Hey Marvin, good to see you. What brings you by?" Aaron asked.

"Looking for a tree, Aaron."

"Are you kidding, what happened to yours?"

"Haven't got one yet."

"Oh bull, you're always one of the first ones here each year. We joke about you getting the pick-of-the-litter." Aaron wore gloves, stocking cap, a heavy flannel shirt and a down vest that looked as if it had been overinflated. He looked positively warm. Marvin shivered across from him.

"Well, I'm just late this year. Let's see what you've got."

"Gee, we're pretty picked over—no litter picks left; that's for sure. We've got some decent shorter Scotch pines, though."

"You know I need a tall one, Aaron. It's a Larson tradition. The vaulted ceiling for the Christmas tree was pretty high on Tina's wish list when we bought the house. We've always had a tall one ever since."

"Not much left, I'm tellin' you. Come on, I'll show you what we got and you can see for yourself." Aaron led him to the far side of the lot.

They approached a handful of tall scrawny spruces scattered among the empty racks where better trees had once stood. He examined the cast-offs. What would Tina think when he came home with one of them? But it wasn't only Tina; a big tree represented his escape from a childhood spent living on the fringes of wealth. His mother had tried hard to give Brad and Deb and him the best life a divorced mother could. She worked two jobs so they could afford an apartment in the Shawnee Mission School District where they had received a first-class secondary education. But living among the wealthy when you weren't, had enormous drawbacks for a child, especially at Christmas time. As a youth, Marvin dealt with equal doses of embarrassment, whether bringing friends over to their spartan apartment, or when visiting the opulence of his friend's homes. And at Christmas time, the inevitable competitive comparisons of "look-what-I-got" left Marvin woefully on the outside.

The thirty-inch, green, artificial tree with pipe cleaner-like branches that his mother lovingly placed on the apartment's coffee table each holiday season epitomized these feelings. Each time any of them watched television, the commercial time was spent fiddling with the wire and fabric branches trying to make it look more treeish and less fake. With no room beneath the tree for even the meager number of gifts they gathered each year, his family placed them on the carpet under the coffee table. He rarely invited anyone over in December. The adolescent Marvin pledged to himself more than once that there would always be a live Christmas tree with presents underneath in his house in December.

From a sparse selection, Marvin selected the least scrawny spruce, about an eight and a half footer.

"What do I owe you for this one Aaron?"

"Heck Marv, I feel bad charging you anything for that pitiful stick, but you know it's for a good cause."

"I do, Boys and Girls clubs again right? How much?"

"Yup, Boys and Girls Clubs of KC. Well, it's six dollars a foot, but I'm only going to charge you for six feet. It's not much more than a spindle above that." Aaron wrapped the tree in plastic mesh.

"I won't short-change the Boys and Girls at Christmas time, Aaron." Marvin reached in his front pocket for his bills. "You know I was one myself once."

"No kidding, Marv. You were a boy and a girl once yourself?" Aaron laughed at his own joke. Marvin smiled, as much at Aaron's joviality as at the remark.

Marvin gave Aaron fifty dollars, told him to keep the change and the two tied the tree into the Buick's trunk. Aaron, a seasonal tree transportation expert, fixed the trunk partially closed with twine and fastened some hot pink surveyor's ribbon to the tip of the tree. Marvin opened the Buick's door and thanked Aaron. Marvin looked back at the tree sticking out behind the car like a possum's tail and hoped Tina and the kids would be okay with it. After all, the tree was plenty tall enough.

When Marvin pulled into the driveway, Trevor came out the front door in his brown canvas Carhartt, wearing leather gloves. Trevor was already taller than Marvin's six feet two inches, and he walked with the confident, slouching gate that seventeen-year-old males seem to have perfected. Marvin opened the Buick's door and climbed out. He noted the Twins at the front picture window watching, their breath clouding up the glass.

"Mom says I'm supposed to help get the tree in." Trevor said with indifferent nonchalance, showing that unlike his sisters jumping up and down at the window, this was no big deal for him. The two met at the trunk and Marvin pulled out his pocketknife and cut away the twine, freeing the trunk lid to pop open. He began wrapping the twine into a ball.

"You gotta be kidding, Dad. That's not a tree; it's a twig."

"Trevor, it's the best they had."

"What, you mean they only had one tree left. Come on, Dad. That tree is sick."

"It'll look fine once we get it decorated. Help me get it out of the trunk."

"That tree will only look fine once it's run through a chipper," Trevor grasped the tip as Marvin reached into the trunk and lifted the base. They carried the spruce

62

to the front door, the hot pink surveyor's ribbon flapping festively behind in the cold north wind—snapping and popping like an anticipatory drum roll, Marvin thought. But anticipating what?

The front door opened as they reached the porch. Inside stood Tina and Brett; Rachael and Francis were still glued to the window. Once in the foyer, Marvin set the base down and Trevor walked his end up until the tree was vertical. It really didn't look like much, Marvin thought. As the family gathered around, Trevor and Brett cut the net away. Scissors rapidly sliced through the netting, revealing the spruce in all its non-glory.

"Oh honey," Tina said.

"Dad, is that a tree or a totem pole?" Brett asked. The Twins stood silent, mouths slightly open, aghast.

"Well, that tree was the only decent tall one," Marvin said; now his feelings were hurt. "It was the best they had except for some really short ones, which I knew you wouldn't want." Marvin looked at Tina for support, but she was silent, looking stricken.

"Give me some money and your keys and I'll find a good one," Trevor said to Marvin.

"We already have a tree," Marvin said. "This one's good enough."

"Mom?" Trevor turned to Tina with his appeal.

"Okay Trevor, take the van. I'll get you some cash." Tina reached for her purse, and she looked back at Marvin, wearing an unspoken apology.

"Who wants to go with me?" Trevor asked, and all of the kids stampeded to the hall closet, rooting around for their coats and gloves.

Marvin turned away, taking off his overcoat as he clumped up the stairs without looking back. In the bedroom, he tossed the coat on the bed, picked up his Cormack McCarthy novel laying on the nightstand. He walked into the master bath, shutting and locking the door. He pulled down his pants, eased himself down on the toilet and opened McCarthy's book to the place marked with one of his realty cards. The bathroom had always been a place to get away, his thinking place. Trevor called it dad's throne room.

He began again, reading about McCarthy's un-named man and boy whose troubles along *The Road* were far worse than his own. Marvin heard Rachael's squeal outside—something about riding in the front seat—followed by the van's doors slamming shut. He heard the engine start. They *were* going to look for another tree. This tree thing and his money troubles didn't compare to the post-apocalyptic world McCarthy's two protagonists struggled through, but his troubles were real, not make believe. As well written and heart rending as *The Road* was, it didn't compare to what he dealt with right here, right now. Tina's soft knock on the door brought him out of the comparative woes of the novel and his life.

"Are you okay in there, honey?" Tina asked through the door.

"I'm fine."

"Well, turn on the exhaust fan then. We don't want to stink up the whole top floor," she chuckled.

"Okay." Marvin read on, and for a while, like with any good book he forgot about his troubles and cloaked himself in McCarthy's novel. After a time, he flushed the toilet, went into the bedroom, dropped on the bed and continued reading. Tina came in and sat at the end of the bed. She slid his left pant leg up and massaged his calf.

"Sorry about the tree, honey. You gotta admit, it really isn't much to look at." Tina smiled in a conciliatory manner.

Marvin snapped, "Do we have to have a perfect tree every year—a perfect tree to match our perfect kids and our perfect life? How spoiled have we become that we can't accept a tree that won't make Martha Stewart's magazine?" Did he really mean that or did he want to hurt Tina's feelings like his had been hurt? But he couldn't stop himself and forged ahead.

"Are we in some kind of glorious Christmas competition? The best lights, the biggest, fullest tree, the most expensive, best-wrapped presents? Time's short; don't we have to hurry up and decorate? Christmas is only five days away; the holiday judges may show up any moment. Quick Tina—bake the cookies and put on the potpourri! Fire up the fricking stereo, dig out the Bing Crosby..."

Tina removed her hand from his calf and held it up in a sign of surrender. Without speaking, she stood and walked from the room. Was that a tear on her cheek?

"Tina! Tina?" She had either gone downstairs out of earshot, or had chosen to ignore him.

Car doors slammed out on the lawn and the clatter of children's laughter filtered through the walls. Marvin heard the front door fly open and bang against the wall. He knew that sound. He heard Tina yell at Brett about how many times he needs to be reminded not to throw the door open. Tina's voice sounded a little shrill and strained. Marvin reopened his book, but he couldn't concentrate. He read the same passage several times without anything soaking in. He listened to the commotion downstairs. The kids sounded proud and happy, and Tina seemed to get caught up in their festive spirit.

Marvin set McCarthy's grim book down and returned to the master bath, removed his clothing, tossing them in a pile in the corner and turned on the shower, setting it as hot as he could stand. He stepped in and slid the glass door shut. For a few moments, the ecstasy of tiny superheated needles of water washed away any thoughts of guilt and debt and trees and the things he had just said to Tina, but only for a few moments. Normally, when Marvin showered a sound track of music played in his head, accompanying the heat and the water and his cleansing actions.

Sometimes he sang along to the soundtrack; last Tuesday it had been *"Either Way"* from the new Wilco CD, and Tina had laughed out loud from the bedroom at his rendition of the chorus. But that was before John Brown, his broker, had phoned about the margin call on his Citigroup investment. Today, no music tracks played for him and the steam rolled around him in accusational silence.

He dried off, pulled on some blue sweats and a KU t-shirt, and was walking to his closet for slippers when he heard a quiet, polite knock on the bedroom door. He would apologize to Tina.

"Come in," he called out, and the door opened. It wasn't Tina, but Rachael and Francis in the doorway.

"We're going to decorate the tree tonight, dad, and we're ready for the lights." Family tradition called for Marvin to string the lights—he did so every year. He was about to decline, to pass the torch to Trevor, when the twins advanced, each taking one of his hands. They led him through the bedroom door and down the stairs. Their hands were small and warm and the firm pressure the girls applied reflected the excitement of eight-year-olds.

When they reached the bottom of the stairs, Marvin observed a tree, already set up in the corner of the family room; it was a beauty, a white pine. Brett and Tina stood with the strings of lights laid out neatly at their feet.

"Not bad, huh?" Trevor slouched on the couch, legs crossed and hands locked behind his neck.

"Very nice, where's the spruce?" Marvin asked.

"We tossed it into the back yard," Trevor said.

Trevor's response stung. Had he become super-sensitive because of his secret: the savings he had tossed away as if it had been a few pennies instead of the tens of thousands of dollars carefully saved over seventeen years? The spruce, now laying out in the yard, had become a bellwether of thoughtless acts—

acts that unintentionally hurt people. But is the pain lessened because of lack of intention?

Marvin shook his head and picked up the strand that ended with the clear white bulb to illuminate the angel. He always started at the top. Francis ran for the stepladder. While they waited, Tina gave him a look that was part sympathy and part something he couldn't decipher. In return, he gave her the best smile he could muster. Francis arrived with the wobbly red and white metal stepladder that had been his mother's—that had been a part of his childhood. She hefted it and presented the ladder to him as if she were presenting a crown to her king. He gave her a half-hearted bow and mounted to begin stringing the lights.

"You're the best tree-lighter-man in the whole world," Rachael told him as he worked his way low enough to discard the ladder. Marvin winked at her. He had to admit, he was pretty accomplished. The trick was not only even spacing around the tree, but moving the lights in and out so there were just as many deep in the interior as around the outside. He felt proud each year, stepping back, knowing only some minor tweaking had to be done—a few of one color too close together, perhaps.

Once he had finished, and the lights glistened in near perfect symmetry on this impressive white pine, he stood aside, per tradition, and the family descended on the tree with ornaments in hand like a plague of Christmas locusts. Trevor reset the ladder and climbed up while Francis handed him ornaments for the high limbs.

Marvin walked to the kitchen and poured a glass of Michael Collins, plopped in a few ice cubes and moved to the back door. He peered through the glass at the spruce laid out like a body on the back lawn and took a sip of the Irish whiskey. Every cell in his body implored him to talk with Tina, air it out, and get it over with, but Marvin ignored the impulse. He turned away from the spruce corpse, and took his drink to the family room where Tina poked around the stereo. Marvin sat in his recliner watching the kids at the tree. Nat King Cole began singing about fire-roasted chestnuts.

Tina approached him and carefully sat on his lap, taking the drink from his hand. She took a sip, shook her head and stuck her tongue out.

"Yuck." She handed back the drink, stood and returned to the boxes of ornaments. "Gingerbread cookies after dinner everybody," she said. God, he loved her.

He sat at his fancy cherry desk, once again watching the sparse traffic through the trees, people running final errands on Christmas Eve. Marvin had already phoned to sell their "college" mutual funds, and he had also left a voice mail for John Brown, informing him the margin call funds would be transferred on the twenty-seventh, fulfilling his debt obligations for now. He didn't really need to be in his office today; he could have made the calls from home. Nothing else here needed doing. He was hiding, using the office as a remote version of dad's throne room. Someone else worked here today as well—he could hear Johnny Mathis sappily singing about jingling sleigh bells just down the hall.

The golf clock clanged four times, disrupting his reverie, as if his clock was a harbinger of some Christmas ghost who would be walking through the wall at the last chime. He had to suck-it-up, put on his Christmas face and head home. Snow flurries—no accumulation—had been forecast and flakes floated down as he walked across the lot to his car. The strong winds of the last few days had moved on, allowing the tiny flakes to drift aimlessly, immune to gravity, like dust particles in a beam of sunlight.

Marvin pulled into his subdivision, Longhurst Forest, at a quarter-to-five. Larson tradition called for a Christmas Eve glazed ham dinner at six. Afterward they would gather around the tree and each family member would open a single present, saving the rest for Christmas morning. Tina and Marvin always made sure the younger children opened something to occupy them until bedtime, a game or a toy. Sweaters or socks just wouldn't do on Christmas Eve.

Marvin turned into his driveway. Streaking snowflakes framed in the yellow porch light signified the wind had picked up. A rainbow of colors twinkled in the white pine behind the family room window as he came up the walk. It snowed harder now, with bigger flakes. On the porch Marvin reached for the doorknob, but the door opened inward. Rachael stood there glowing, in navy slacks and a red Christmas tree embroidered sweater, her auburn hair tied back in a ponytail with a red ribbon.

"Mom says you just have time for a shower if you hurry. She said to tell you that you must scoot up the stairs as quick as you can because we don't want any stinky present openers." She beamed at him, pleased to remember the message verbatim.

"Okay sweetie, tell mom I'm scooting," Marvin rubbed the top of Rachael's head and started for the stairs.

Once again no music track played for him in the shower. Instead he felt the scalding hot stream of guilt and fifty thousand dollars of recrimination. How could he feel any joy when he had virtually destroyed his family's future? Once out of the shower and dressed, an apparition of gloom accompanied him as he walked through the bedroom door and down the stairs. Brett and Francis were setting the dinner table. "Just in time, Dad," Francis said. "We're almost ready. Mom's getting the rolls out of the oven."

Marvin remained unusually quiet at dinner, contrasting the lively discussion around him. At one point, Tina raised an eyebrow and gave him an unintelligible smile from across the table, to which he responded with a shrug of his shoulders. The meal appeared to be delicious from the way his family devoured it, but Marvin had lost both his appetite and his sense of taste. He ate mechanically and refused the seconds offered him.

After dinner they gathered around the tree. Distracted, Marvin sat down in his recliner while Tina announced that this year presents would be opened in reverse order of the family's ages, beginning with the twins. Marvin paid only partial attention. He half watched the twins open their *American Girls* books and dolls, and by the time Brett opened his *Halo 3* game, Marvin decided that he would talk with Tina on the day after Christmas about his investment blunder. He promised himself that he would not put it off any further, and the promise itself brought him a modicum of relief. Trevor opened his gift, a leather bomber's jacket from mom and dad, and Tina's present from the twins revealed a Christmas tree sweater almost identical to the one Rachael wore.

"It's beautiful," Tina said. "Thank you, Francis and Rachael." Tina pulled the sweater on over her white button-down blouse and spun around and around like a runway model, to the delight of the girls.

"Okay, it's time for dad's present. Everybody ready?" Tina said. Each member of the family ran off in a different direction. When they returned, they all had coats and hats on. Brett held Marvin's beat-up London Fog, Rachael carried his gloves and Trevor had a bandana. Francis walked up to him, took his hands in hers, "Get up, Dad."

Brett helped him on with the London Fog, Rachael held out his gloves one at a time for him to put on, and Trevor asked him to turn around. Once he turned, Trevor blindfolded him with the bandana. Francis and Rachael, each taking one of his gloved hands, led him through the house, walking slowly and carefully. Obviously something outside. Perhaps the Brinkmann smoker he'd told Tina about. They led him out a door.

He could feel the cold wind and snowflakes melting on his neck and cheeks. The girls stopped him, and someone untied his blindfold.

They stood in the backyard. Before him towered the sparse spruce, now standing tall, it glowed with myriad colored lights. Garlands of popcorn and colored paper rings encircled it from top to bottom and snow rested on the tips of its branches.

"It was Francis' idea. Tell dad about it, dear," Tina said.

"Well, I knew we made you feel bad about the tree, Dad. We hurt your feelings. And I was outside Saturday looking at the tree and it reminded me of Mary and Joseph, and how no one in Bethlehem would let them come inside, and so Jesus had to be born in a stable. But even though they were stuck outside, people started bringing Him presents, the shepherds and the wise men, and everybody."

"So we brought the tree presents," Rachael continued.

"Trevor and I made a stand and anchored it in the ground to keep the tree from falling over," Brett said.

"And Trevor hung the lights," Rachael added. "He's almost as good a tree-lighter-man as you are, Dad."

"Brett and Mom strung popcorn and Rachael and I made ribbons of green and red construction paper and we used two whole roles of scotch tape," Francis said. "We did it for you, Dad, and for Jesus, because it's his birthday. Jesus said we should be nice to people and love them. We wanted to be nice to you and show you that we love you, so you won't feel bad anymore."

"We do love you, you know," Trevor said.

Marvin's voice wavered, "Kids, this means so much to me, more than you know. You couldn't have given a better present."

Tina came up behind Marvin and put her arms around his chest and kissed his neck and gazed at the tree, her chin tilted up and resting on his shoulder.

They all stood motionless watching the scrawny, spectacular tree glowing in the falling snow, blotting out the night's darkness.

"Why don't you kids go inside and make us some hot chocolate? I want a few minutes alone with your mother."

"Come on guys, let's go heat up some cocoa." Trevor said.

"With marshmallows?" Francis asked.

"Sure, why not?" The children filed through the kitchen door.

Marvin turned around to face Tina, placed his hands on her hips and looked into her eyes. "Tina, there's something I need to tell you."

"Honey..."

"No, Tina, I need to say this."

Tina put her hand on Marvin's chest and said, "Honey, John Brown called today to say he got your voice mail and that the twenty-seventh would be fine. We had a long talk."

"Oh Tina, I'm so sorry. I just..."

Tina moved her hand up to his lips. "Shh," she said. "It's just money. And it's not like we're destitute. You've got four great kids who love you, and I think I love you more every day. We're gonna be okay. I told Mr. Brown—he seems like a nice man—I told him that we would talk to him after the first of the year about what we need to do or pay to get out of this margin thing. We'll be okay."

Marvin held her tight. The snow melting on his cheeks mingled with his tears. They remained together, hugging, wordless for some time. Tina, on tiptoes, whispered in his ear, "Let's go inside, drink some cocoa and enjoy our Two-Tree Christmas."

Marvin smiled. He didn't think he would be coming up with his own secret name this year. Two-Tree was perfect. He kissed Tina's forehead and then her lips and took her hand. As Tina opened the back door, Marvin turned for one more look at his sparse spruce gift. He noticed a crystal clear light expertly placed at the top of the tree, and just below it, the pink surveyor's ribbon flapped festively in the cold north wind—snapping and popping like an anticipatory drum roll—anticipating the birth of a child who would change everything.

Open Seven Days a Week, Except Mondays

–1–

Malcolm Blanding lived a life of precision, a good thing, because Malcolm was a precise person—order in everything and everything in its proper order. Life was good.

Though thirty-three, Malcolm lived alone. And that was precisely how he wanted it. He had passed beyond the economic need for a roommate, thank God. Too often other people failed him, pushed him into the randomness he despised.

Women were worst of all. Though Malcolm was not a biblical person, he could almost believe women had been touched by the Devil way back in the Garden— that they were placed on Earth to befuddle men and to dispense chaos.

Not only did Malcolm live alone, he had secured a position that allowed him to work from home, on his own timetable, and without the presence of huddled masses of annoying humanity. He worked as a commercial website editor for numerous companies and professional organizations.

Malcolm liked his life, a life that had become as comfortable as an old pair of slippers. Order in a chaotic world was tough to produce, and even tougher to maintain, as he was about to find out.

–2–

Every Thursday evening between six-thirty and six-forty-five Malcolm walked the five blocks from his Chicago apartment building to the Hunan Rice House, where he ate cashew chicken and drank one Tsingtao beer. He ate the whole meal, so there was no need to destroy the environment by encouraging use of Styrofoam to-go containers.

His Thursday Rice House meal varied once each year. On Thanksgiving, in a nod to their new American home, the Lim family substituted turkey for chicken dishes.

And that's when this story began—Thanksgiving Day.

On that Thanksgiving Day, Malcolm opened the Rice House's menu and smiled at the bold letters at the top of each page, **Open Seven Days a Week, Except Mondays**. Though the Lims spoke English well, they still had a way to go. Malcolm chuckled. Maybe he could branch out and do Chinese restaurant menu editing as well.

"Happy Thanksgiving, Mr. Blanding. You want cashew turkey and Tsingtao?"

"Happy Thanksgiving, Mr. Lim." Malcolm closed the menu. He liked Mr. Lim. Mr. Lim knew how to appreciate order and precision. "That would be correct."

Mr. Lim laughed and held a hand up as if he were pointing to heaven. "I had hunch that what you order."

Malcolm laughed too, and extended his arms. "An open book, Mr. Lim."

"Your order come right up." He turned and retreated to the kitchen.

Though Malcolm lived a precise life, he was not picky. He had never told Mr. Lim that he didn't much care for turkey dark meat. Each year—this was his fifth Rice House Thanksgiving—Malcolm surveyed his cashew turkey, estimating the percentage of dark to white.

When his meal came, preceded by the Tsingtao and a spotless glass, Malcolm waited until Mr. Lim had turned to address the only other occupied table. As Mr. Lim spoke to the Asian-looking couple vociferously and his arms waving frenetically, Malcolm inspected the entrée. He frowned, disappointed at high percentage of dark meat. Sixty percent dark established a new, negative Thanksgiving Day record. Nevertheless he cleaned his plate, and though the meat wasn't all white, it wasn't all that bad. *Waste not; want not,* his father used to say.

While Malcolm ate, Mr. Lim returned.

"How is cashew turkey?"

"Very tasty, thank you." Malcolm didn't mention the troublesome dark meat.

Then Mr. Lim asked the question he always asked, even though he knew how Malcolm would respond.

"You like another Tsingtao?"

"No, thanks. The check will be fine."

Mr. Lim nodded as if a wobble in the Earth's revolution had righted itself, and, sedulous now, Earth had returned to its proper orbit and place in the universe. A few minutes later Mr. Lim returned with the check and a cellophane wrapped fortune cookie.

Mrs. Lim shouted something Chinese from the kitchen, and Mr. Lim, voice raised, shouted back unintelligibly, smiled, and rolled his eyes at Malcolm, then hurried off.

Malcolm placed a twenty on the tray—his meal and a generous tip, the same tip he always left—and opened the fortune cookie. This cookie was fresh and crisp. Sometimes they were not. Then Malcolm looked at the fortune. He looked for a long time. No wonder. His fortune read, *Come back tomorrow evening for a dinner that will change your life.*

Someone had obviously pranked him. Malcolm looked around for the Lims, or a bus boy, anyone who might be playing a joke. But the few people there all went about their business, oblivious to what transpired at his table.

Malcolm believed logic was necessary to an ordered life. It was logical that a prank had been played. Because the cellophane had not been broken, the prank must have been perpetrated at the factory that produced the fortune cookies. He dismissed the notion it might be a marketing ploy to attract return business—not logical. It would only anger people when they returned and nothing changed in their lives.

He called out a goodbye and happy Thanksgiving to Mr. and Mrs. Lim chattering away in the kitchen in fast incomprehensible Chinese.

At home, as was his habit on Thursdays, Malcolm picked up the book he'd been reading intending as usual to read for precisely one hour. That Thanksgiving night, he read the latest James Lee Burke novel. Dave Robicheaux, Burke's southern Louisiana detective protagonist, was far from a precise or orderly man, even though he often employed feats of logic. And that was why he enjoyed Burke's books. A life of precision for Malcolm was as much a necessity as oxygen. But he often imagined other lives, the New Orleans detective, or the Portland cop hero in his favorite TV show, *Grimm.* Malcolm was no Walter Mitty, but escape in carefully measured doses was not an unhealthful thing.

After finishing chapter nine Malcolm looked at his watch. He still had sixteen minutes of reading left. But his work on the Kansas Recreation and Parks Association website neared completion.

Malcolm liked to invent clever confidential acronyms for his clients, in this case, KRAPA. Maybe he could finish the website project that night. If so, he would read sixteen minutes into Burke's chapter ten afterward.

Malcolm set the book on the end table next to his easy chair in precisely the same place he always did. He walked across the room to his home office. Before he took the seat at his personal computer he noticed a small slip of paper centered on the keyboard below the Y and above the H. It had the crease from having been folded once. On the slip was printed the words, *Come back tomorrow evening for a dinner that will change your life.*

–3–

Odd. Malcolm felt sure he had left the fortune on his table at the Hunan. And he was relatively certain he hadn't approached his PC since returning. But any alternative explanation defied logic. He had experienced a memory lapse—the only rational possibility. Why would he have placed the fortune on his keyboard? A question for another time.

Malcolm picked up the fortune, folded it twice, and tossed it in the kitchen trash as he entered to make a pot of decaffeinated coffee. While the pot brewed he returned to the PC and opened the KRAPA professional certification protocol. He worked until the coffeemaker ceased gurgling and then retrieved a cup, adding precisely one level teaspoon of pure cane sugar from Hawaii.

Back at the PC, Malcolm worked meticulously for thirty minutes. At the thirty-minute mark he returned to the kitchen and procured a second cup, exacting the same measure of sugar. Malcolm estimated he would complete his KRAPA work in time to read for sixteen minutes and still slide into bed by ten.

Malcolm reached his work station and what he saw caused him to slosh half his sugar-enriched coffee on his chair and the surrounding emerald-green, deep-pile carpet. There, nestled between the Y and the H was his fortune with a single crease. The fortune contained no evidence of the message having been folded a second time, only the single pristine fold.

Impossible. Malcolm spilled half the remaining coffee as he ran into the kitchen. He rifled through the trash receptacle, throwing trash hither and yon. No fortune. He searched the debris on the kitchen floor a second time. No fortune. Malcolm sat on the linoleum in the midst of six days of strewn refuse. He would mentally try to retrace his actions. Before he began, the logical Malcolm, the real Malcolm, suggested he return and look again—this time without a mug of coffee.

–4–

The fortune remained perfectly centered, as if a scrupulous person had carefully placed it. The slip possessed a single crease. Malcolm reached down and touched a corner, half expecting an electrical shock. Nothing. He lifted it by that same corner carefully, as if it were a dead, lice-infested bird he'd found outside on his balcony.

Malcolm dropped it in the kitchen sink and reached into a drawer for his box of Fire Chief Strike Anywhere matches. He swiped one on the stainless steel sink trim and set the note on fire, then watched it burn completely. Malcolm turned on the faucet, grabbed the spray nozzle, turned on the garbage disposal, and blasted the sink until every trace of ash had disappeared. "There," he said.

Under the sink he retrieved what he needed to clean the carpet and the chair, and returned to his PC—no note there, nothing out of place except the stains. Twenty minutes later he was back at the KRAPA protocol, sitting on a trash bag to insulate him from the chair's wet fabric. But he couldn't concentrate. He'd had a scare, and anyone in his right mind would have trouble concentrating. Malcolm, perhaps more than anyone, felt assured he *was indeed* in his right mind.

Malcolm abandoned KRAPA, returned to his easy chair, and picked up Dave Robicheaux in a tavern on the outskirts of New Orleans. But he found himself reading the same half-page over and over without anything soaking in. His mind strayed to the fortune and what must have been his uncharacteristic behavior and forgetfulness. One thing was certain. He would *not* be going to dinner at the Hunan Rice House on Friday.

Every Friday at six forty Malcolm phoned Pizza Hut delivery and ordered a medium, thin-crust pizza with

Italian sausage, pepperoni, green peppers and mushrooms, accompanied by a small order of garlic bread. At seven he turned on his television and watched *Grimm.* Sometime around the first commercial break his order arrived. Malcolm then ate half his pizza and half of the garlic bread during the program, saving the remainder of each for lunch on Saturday. If there was one immutable pleasure to the organization of his existence it was Friday evenings with pizza and *Grimm.* Any tricks, or sleight of hand, fortune cookie mumbo jumbo that some disharmonious corner of his brain might be perpetrating would fail. He would have his pizza and *Grimm.*

Malcolm looked at his wristwatch. It was just over an hour before ten-thirty, his routine bedtime. He could not work. He could not read. The rhythm of his life had been upset by a silly fortune cookie. Order now disordered, he did what the huddled masses would do. He turned on the television. The program portrayed some modern day Sherlock Holmes performing feats of faux logic amidst the chaos of crime in New York City. It kept him amused just enough to push the fortune out of his thoughts.

The program ended and his set suggested he stay tuned for previews of next week's exciting episode of *Elementary.* Instead Malcolm switched it off. He looked around his living room. Plain would be a kind word to describe it. The street-side, on which his balcony had been constructed, and the wall on the opposite side of the room were painted a shade of not-quite-white. The semi-transparent curtain to the balcony's sliding door— now closed—was lemon chiffon to complement the walls that led to the bedroom and the kitchen with his adjacent office. Those walls had been painted cheery yellow by a former resident.

Other than the lone curtain the walls held no trappings, no wall coverings, no paintings, no photos, no family portraits—not even one of his mother, who, unlike his father, he had loved very much. His mother's death when he was eleven taught him a hard lesson. Life is not fair. Life left the eleven-year-old with his father, a disciplinarian kindly put.

When Malcolm's mother died the buffer she had placed between her love and his father's rigidity had been removed. Malcolm's father laid out a draconian set of rules that must not be brooked. He also set harsh and escalating consequences for failure to comply. Malcolm spent the remainder of his childhood, not in a home, but in a penitentiary with his father as warden.

With a full academic scholarship to Purdue, Malcolm left his prison in August of 1998 and never returned. He wished he had taken a portrait of his mother, one he could hang on his barren walls, one he could look at every morning and begin each day with a smile and a pleasant memory. But he would not ask for one, nor set foot in that prison of a house until his father was dead and in the ground.

Malcolm shook off such thoughts and, after washing his face, brushing his teeth thirty-five circular strokes on both the uppers and lowers, went to bed. He could not sleep. But Malcolm wasn't surprised after the odd day he had.

As he lay awake replaying the evening's odd occurrences, he recalled reading Charles Dickens' *A Christmas Carol* from the school library as a teenager. Though Dickens' Scrooge was not confronted with reappearing bizarre cookie fortunes, he did see the ghost of his partner.

You may be an undigested bit of beef, a blot of mustard, a crumb of cheese, a fragment of an underdone potato. There's more of gravy than of grave about you, whatever you are! Scrooge said to the ghostly image of Marley.

Perhaps that was the case here—too much underdone turkey dark meat.

Malcolm eventually slept. He slept well. He didn't receive visits from three ghosts. But his story wasn't over.

–5–

When Malcolm woke Friday morning he had forgotten the fortune. But he remembered as he showered, in the midst of his complex ritual of bathing. After drying—yes, another complex ritual involving a towel folded into quarters—Malcolm put on his Hanes, left leg first, and slipped on slippers.

With no small amount of apprehension he walked directly to his office. He fixed his eyes on the computer keyboard. No fortune. He proceeded to the kitchen. No fortune on the counter or in the sink. He checked the top layer of trash in the kitchen basket.

Nothing. Malcolm sighed, relieved.

He prepared one level cup of quick oats. Once the oatmeal was heated and ready Malcolm sprinkled on raisins and stirred them in. No, he did not count the raisins—a half-handful, more or less, sufficed. While Malcolm ate, and as he prepared mentally to complete the KRAPA certification protocol, a thought wormed its way into his consciousness. The fortune had replaced his bookmark in the Burke novel. The thought itself was preposterous. He dismissed it.

Or rather he tried to dismiss it.

But the thought refused rejection. He knew the fortune lay wedged between page 178 and 179. Frustrated with himself and an inability to properly reason, Malcolm abandoned the half-eaten oatmeal and raisins. He walked to the living room, lifted the book, and opened it to the marked page.

His place was held by the same Book Owl Store marker he had placed there the night before. Malcolm flipped through all of the pages just to make sure the fortune didn't lurk elsewhere.

After breakfast he carried his first cup of coffee into the adjacent office. Despite a conscious effort not to, his gaze traveled immediately to his keyboard. Nothing there except keys.

Malcolm spent nearly three hours finishing a protocol that should have taken less than half that time. The fortune stuck with him—niggling—demanding attention. His brow furrowed as he worked. His jaw clenched, softened, and clenched again. His fingers refused to cooperate with the keys. The more he struggled to excommunicate the previous day's occurrences, the more they refused excommunication.

Normally, he worked until three on Friday afternoons. But his concentration was shot by noon. Malcolm made one peanut butter and grape jam sandwich, carefully smoothing the peanut butter and molding the jam. He selected five celery stalks from the refrigerator and ate lunch.

Suddenly very tired, Malcolm lay down on the couch after lunch. He quickly fell asleep, another detour from his routine. Malcolm did not take naps.

He did not recall dreaming, but upon awakening he felt uneasy, as if he'd had broad-daylight nightmares. Malcolm made another trip through his apartment looking for the fortune. Satisfied the slip of paper had not miraculously reappeared, Malcolm poured himself a half-glass of orange juice and sat at the kitchen table.

He sipped the juice and assessed his emotional state—jittery and angry, two emotions he rarely experienced. That silly fortune cookie had disrupted his life. He must put the silliness to rest.

–6–

At six forty-five a somewhat frazzled Malcolm Blanding began his five-block trek to the Hunan Rice House. The Friday traffic, both foot and vehicular, was much heavier than his accustomed Thursday ventures. Everyone hurried, horns honked, pedestrians walked rapidly, jostling one another. Malcolm maintained his normal pace, his shoes purposefully avoiding the troweled seams and expansion joints in the sidewalk.

When Malcolm arrived, a dozen people stood around the register. An attractive girl who couldn't be more than sixteen leaned over the register. "How many in your party, sir?"

Party? It took a moment for the question to register. "Oh, it's just me."

"It will be about thirty minutes. Would you care to wait?"

"Um. I don't know. I guess so."

"May I have your name?"

"Huh?"

She pointed to the sheet on the counter. "For the waiting list."

"Oh, Blanding, Malcolm J."

"Okay, Mr. Blanding, we'll call your name when your table is ready."

Malcolm retreated into the corner behind the front door next to an older man and woman who snuggled like teenagers. Moments later an obese couple entered with two pre-adolescent children—a boy and girl both working toward obesity. The father gave his name to the girl and the family backed into Malcolm's corner.

This whole trip was a mistake. Malcolm felt claustrophobic. The boy, now only inches from him, smelled bad and relentlessly picked at the seat of his pants. The older couple seemed oblivious to it all. To calm himself Malcolm tried his Zen breathing exercises.

Mr. Lim approached the front counter, said something to the girl who grabbed menus then called out someone's name, finishing with "party of four." As she and her group headed deep into the restaurant, Mr. Lim took a look at her list. His eyes rose from the paper and surveyed those waiting. He found Malcolm.

"Mr. Blanding! You wait. I find place. I squeeze you in."

Malcolm nodded his thanks. Mr. Lim bowed and hurried off. The large couple stared at Malcolm as if he had just robbed a Quick Trip. He retreated farther into the corner, his back against the storefront glass.

The children began to complain. They were hungry. Why did they have to wait so long. Their parents should have taken them to Hardees like *they* had wanted. Or McDonalds. The parents shouted and threatened. Threatened and shouted. The father raised his hand at his son as if he would give him a backhanded smack.

Malcolm touched his cheek. He recalled the sting of his father's backhand, a sharp pain he would never forget. Yet this man did not follow through as Malcolm's father so often had. The children's misbehaving escalated. Even the man and woman next to Malcolm ceased snuggling.

Why people would ever decide to have children escaped Malcolm. Children were demanding, self-centered apes who spent their young lives tormenting adults. They must be dealt with sternly, must be made to toe the line. A good swat in the face would have quieted that boy.

"Mr. Blanding. Mr. Blanding! Your table ready. You come." Mr. Lim waived a menu at him.

Malcolm tried to slide his way out of the corner without touching anyone. The older couple looked at him as if they stood on the *Titanic's* deck and he was the last to board the last lifeboat. He had almost navigated his way through the icy waters when the male child stepped back, brushing his well-picked bottom firmly on Malcolm's thighs.

I'll have to dry clean these pants, Malcolm thought. Or throw them out. He followed Mr. Lim through the restaurant. Malcolm noticed he was perspiring. He reached into his back left pocket for his handkerchief. It was not there. How could he have forgotten? It felt as if any moment droplets of sweat would drip into his eyes. He wiped his brow with his shirtsleeve.

Mr. Lim arrived at a booth and placed the menu down, gesturing for Malcolm. But a mistake had been made.

–7–

Across the booth sat a woman and a toddler who sat on a plastic riser in order to reach the table top.

"I'm sorry, Mr. Lim. You must have made a mistake. Where is my table?"

"No mistake. I squeeze you in. You sit here."

"No. No. I don't even know these people."

The woman looked up at Malcolm with an odd expression.

Malcolm looked at his watch. "I'll just wait for a table for one."

"No table for one. You sit here." Mr. Lim grabbed Malcolm's shirt sleeve. Malcolm thought it was the first time Mr. Lim had ever touched him.

Mr. Lim tugged on his cuff. "You sit. You sit." He tugged harder.

Malcolm sat.

"Mei Ling come take your order," Mr. Lim said, then disappeared into the crowd.

Though the restaurant was noisy, silence hung over Malcolm's table. The woman across the table watched him, but he lowered his head and concentrated on the menu.

"I'm this many."

Malcolm looked up. The little tow-headed girl held the three fingers of her right hand toward him.

"That's three. You're three years old, Sweetheart." The woman patted the child's shoulder and then held out her hand to Malcolm. "Hello. I'm Jennifer Pearson. People call me Jenny."

Malcolm hesitated, then shook her hand perfunctorily. "Good evening, Mrs. Pearson. I'm Malcolm Blanding."

The little girl pointed at Malcolm. "You're sweating."

"April! That's not nice to say."

"He is, Momma."

"But you don't say that to people." She turned away from the girl and looked at Malcolm. She blushed crimson. "Mr. Blanding, this is my daughter, April. Now, April, tell Mr. Blanding you are sorry."

"I'm sorry you're all sweaty, Mr. Blandy."

"April."

The little girl looked at her mother and then at Malcolm. "Sorry."

Malcolm unwrapped his dinnerware. "That's all right, little girl. I am perspiring." Malcolm dabbed at his brow.

"See, Momma."

"April."

"Sorry."

Ignoring the girl and her mother, Malcolm stared at his menu even though he knew he would order the cashew chicken—that is if he didn't decide to leave without ordering. He contemplated just such a thing.

Had Mei Ling arrived sixty seconds later our story would have ended here.

–8–

"Good evening, may I take your drink order?" Mei Ling said in impeccable English, with only a slight Chinese accent. "Here you are, young lady. Would you like to work on this?" Mei Ling placed a small coloring book and five crayons in a Ziploc bag on the table in front of April.

"Oh boy!" April snatched the book while Mrs. Pearson opened the Ziplock.

She placed the crayons on the table for April. "What do you say?"

"Thank you, Momma."

"No, to the nice lady who brought them."

"Thank you, Nice Lady."

Both Mei Ling and Mrs. Pearson laughed. And Malcolm felt his own lips involuntarily stretch, cheek muscles turning them upward at the ends.

Malcolm requested a Tsingtao beer and a glass. Mrs. Pearson asked for hot tea, and milk for April.

"Are you ready to order your meal now, or would you like more time?"

Malcolm wanted out of there as quickly as possible. "I'll have the cashew chicken," he blurted out. Both Mrs. Pearson and Mei Ling looked surprised at the rapid and vociferous manner in which he made his selection.

Jenny bent over the menu. Malcolm thought she appeared panicked at the notion of placing an immediate order.

"I'm sorry, Mrs. Pearson, did you need more time?" Malcolm spoke just before Mei Ling could voice the same question.

"No, that's okay," Mrs. Pearson said, her face inches from the menu. She looked up at him, irritation evident in her eyes though her smile belied it. "And it's Ms. Pearson." She turned to Mei Ling.

"We'll share an order of Moo Shu chicken. And please bring April a small bowl of white rice."

"Separate checks?" Both Malcolm and Ms. Pearson nodded. Mei Ling bowed and hurried off.

Over Ms. Pearson's shoulder Malcolm saw the family with the bratty kids being led to the far end of the restaurant—a stroke of good fortune.

"Mooshu, mooshu, what's a mooshu?" The little girl babbled.

Ms. Pearson smiled. She had a nice smile. A winning smile. "You remember when we had burritos?"

The small girl nodded as Malcolm fidgeted, not knowing what to do with his hands or voice. His left foot quietly tapped out some nearly forgotten rhythm underneath the table.

"And remember I said that people in Mexico ate burritos? And I showed you where Mexico was on the globe?"

Another nod.

"Moo Shu is like a Chinese burrito, only they bring all of the stuffings and we make our own right here at the table."

"You're teasing."

"No, sweetheart, I'm not."

The little girl looked at her mother and then Malcolm. "Momma teases a lot, Mr. Blandy. She's teasing isn't she?"

A memory bubbled to the surface, long suppressed. Malcolm's mother used to tease him. At any moment his mother might initiate the game by saying something outlandish, like Chinese burritos. Often she teased him. But just as often she spoke the truth, and through the game she taught Malcolm wondrous things. What might his life been like had she not died so young.

His father used other methods of teaching, requiring strict obedience and fear of consequences. Malcolm learned from both his mother and his father, and overall, he was happy with the end product.

Malcolm looked up at Ms. Pearson. She watched him with a conspiratorial smile that touched all the corners of her face.

"I don't know if she's teasing or not. I've never eaten Moo Shu." And it was true. Malcolm knew nothing about the dish.

With all of the attention span of a three year-old, the girl reached both hands across the table toward Malcolm. Her right hand held the same carefully positioned three fingers, and her left displayed her forefinger. "Soon I'll be this many."

"That's four, Sweetheart. You will be four on Christmas Eve."

"I was born the day before Jesus."

Ms. Pearson laughed, but did not correct her daughter.

Malcolm thought of how his father might have sternly and physically corrected this girl's blasphemy, public restaurant or not.

The girl busied herself coloring. It appeared she did not even attempt to stay inside the lines. The mother watched her daughter. Malcolm watched the two of them, trying not to be obvious.

Malcolm surveyed the restaurant. He'd never seen it so crowded, and he wondered if all Rice House Fridays were like this.

His gaze returned to the table. Ms. Pearson had her arm around the girl. Both peered down at the coloring book and giggled. Malcolm almost smiled.

Mei Ling arrived. She set the Tsingtao and a glass spotted with one large fingerprint—a thumbprint, Malcolm thought—down in front of him. Malcolm hoped the print was on the outside of the glass. As Malcolm pondered the print—something Lim would never sanction—the young server placed a teacup and saucer, and a small teapot before Ms. Pearson. Finally she set a full glass of milk in front the girl.

Before the girl had a chance to touch the glass, the mother snatched it and drank it down by a third. Malcolm wondered for a moment why Ms. Pearson didn't order her own. Then he understood.

The girl set her crayon down, grasped the glass with both hands, and precariously raised it to her lips. She gulped twice and carefully set the glass down. She looked at her mother and smiled with a milk moustache.

Ms. Pearson nodded. "Good job, sweetheart."

Malcolm tested the print smudge on his glass, confirming that it was on the outside. Were the restaurant not so crowded he would have asked for another. Instead, he turned the smudged side away from him, so his lips would not touch that side of the glass. He expertly poured the beer, carefully approximating the desired one inch of frothy head.

"Do you eat here often?" It was Ms. Pearson who spoke as Malcolm tasted his first sip.

"I come on Thursdays."

"Often?"

"Yes. On Thursdays." Malcolm felt very uneasy and awkward speaking to the woman. He wished they would hurry with his cashew chicken so he could eat in peace.

"This is our first time."

Malcolm did not know if the statement required a response from him. He took a large gulp of Tsingtao, then examined his nails.

"This is April's first fling with Chinese food." She paused, lost in thought, and then she smiled. "She did have a bite of egg roll once. That didn't turn out well at all."

The woman looked at Malcolm. Her eyes glittered, he assumed with the memory of the egg roll tasting. Her face indicated that she was waiting for a response; her eyebrows rose in expectation.

Malcolm tried to think of what he might say. Without any advance planning, his voice responded. "I don't care much for egg rolls either. I expect when I was your daughter's age I made that abundantly clear."

Ms. Pearson laughed. Yes, she did have a nice laugh.

Malcolm's mother would have laughed.

Later, Malcolm learned when it came to food, likes and dislikes were unimportant. You ate everything served to you, the penalties for non-compliance increasingly severe. Malcolm quickly learned there was nothing he wouldn't eat. Many foods he first thought distasteful he learned to like.

The woman struggled to make conversation. Malcolm, responding with minimal words and syllables struggled to be left alone. At some point she abandoned her efforts and supervised her daughter's colorful scorched-earth ride through the coloring book.

Malcolm watched the nearby diners, careful not to appear to be watching. Underneath the table his thumbs twiddled and a foot tapped. No sign of the fat family—good. Occasionally his eyes revisited the mother and daughter across from him. They smiled and giggled and took turns coloring the book's contents.

The young waitress returned with a helper carrying a large tray. From it she lifted Malcolm's cashew chicken and placed it before him. She added the rice bowl, placing it to the right of the entrée. Malcolm slid it over to the left side situated at ten o'clock. She placed an empty plate and a small rice bowl in front of the little girl. Looking at Malcolm, the girl repositioned her rice bowl to mirror his and she nodded her head.

Malcolm smiled.

Mei Ling set down a plate of what she called pancakes—they looked more like tortillas—then a plate of chicken and vegetables, and a small bowl of plum sauce. With aplomb—and chopsticks—she spread chicken-vegetable mix along one side of the pancake. Mei Ling lifted the plum sauce and deftly drizzled a small stripe along the vegetable mix. With chopsticks in her expert hands, she rolled the pancake around the concoction. She and her helper bowed to applause from the mother and daughter.

Throughout the demonstration, Malcolm's attention skittered between mother and child and the amazing demonstration of chopstick dexterity.

"Would you care for another Tsingtao?" Mei Ling asked.

Malcolm was about to respond in the negative when he noticed his glass was empty. How odd. "Yes, please," he heard himself say.

She and her helper hurried off.

Malcolm cleared the upper left corner of his plate and place four spoonfuls of rice there. He began eating, mixing the rice and cashew chicken a forkful at a time.

Across the table Ms. Pearson, cut the end of the "Chinese burrito" off and offered April her first bite.

"Yum, I like it!"

While they shared, Malcolm dug into his dish in earnest. He noticed he was hurrying. A part of him, the seldom heard from illogical part, longed to linger.

Another server brought Malcolm's second Tsingtao and a fresh, spotless glass. He placed the bills on two plates, one before Malcolm with one fortune cookie, and one before Ms. Pearson with two fortune cookies.

"You can pay your server when she returns."

Malcolm poured hurriedly not minding the excess foam. Across the table they were constructing a second burrito using a fork in place of chopsticks. Together mother and daughter rolled it up. Still watching, Malcolm took a deep drink and surreptitiously wiped the foam on his upper lip with his tongue.

"Can I have this one?" April asked. "And can I hold it and eat it like a burrito."

Malcolm observed Ms. Pearson ponder the question.

"I suppose so. But be careful. And lean over your plate when you eat." Ms. Pearson slid the Moo Shu pancake onto her daughter's plate. "And just eat from one end."

"Why, Momma?"

"The contents won't squirt out as much. Hold it with one hand on the end you're not eating from and the other just above the middle."

Intelligent woman, Malcolm thought.

Malcolm watched as the girl began to eat. She held it just as her mother suggested. Malcolm had almost finished his meal. He felt both glad to be nearly done with this uncomfortable encounter and sad that it was about to end.

He was pondering those conflicting emotions when it happened.

–9–

As Malcolm finished the last of his cashew chicken, Ms. Pearson constructed a third "Chinese burrito." April set down her Moo Shu and reached for her milk. Only April—not yet four years old and limited in her coordination and dexterity—wasn't paying a lot of attention.

She knocked her milk glass over toward Malcolm. Her milk glass knocked Malcolm's beer glass over toward Malcolm.

Before Malcolm could say "Jack Robinson" a river of Tsingtao and milk poured onto his lap. Instinctively, Malcolm tried to jump to his feet, banging his thighs on the table which dropped him back down on the booth's bench in time to receive the last of the milk-beer mixture.

Across from him the Pearsons appeared frozen, their mouths agape, as if they were beginning to sing the Christmas carol about Bethlehem. Malcolm ineffectually dabbed at his crotch with a cheap Rice House paper napkin.

He slid out of the booth and surveyed the damage. His crotch was soaked and the liquid stain ran down one leg in a pattern that resembled the state of Florida. Droplets of milk on his knee could have served as Florida's Keys.

People everywhere stared at him. Some laughed. Ms. Pearson's little girl at the table began to cry. The girl's mother instinctively tried to use her cheap paper napkin to dab the stain on Malcolm's crotch. Malcolm leaped backward, jostling a diner at the booth immediately behind him, knocking the diner's water glass over at that table.

That diner leaped to his feet. Two crotch-stained diners stood back to back. Ms. Pearson now tried to calm her daughter. Malcolm felt as if every eye in the restaurant—in Chicago—watched him. Hastily he picked up his tab and the fortune cookie, sticking the cookie in his shirt pocket. He placed the ticket, a twenty and a five dollar bill on the plate and hurried from the restaurant. He spotted a stricken Mr. Lim watching him as he hurried out the door.

–10–

The five block walk up State Street confirmed Malcolm's suspicion—everyone in Chicago was looking at him, and pointing, and laughing at him. When he tried to cover the stain with his hands he felt even more conspicuous. Though it wasn't cold, he wished he had brought a jacket. As he crossed the State Street Bridge over the Chicago River, a ferry boat passed underneath. Malcolm imagined a tour guide saying "On the bridge to your left you will see a man who wet his pants."

By the time Malcolm reached his apartment he felt more mortified than at any time during the seven years he lived with his father. Inside the lobby he hugged the wall of mailboxes in case anyone came through. He gathered his mail—mostly holiday sale flyers—and stepped into the elevator, which mercifully was empty. Included in the mail was an envelope from his father that undoubtedly was a another holiday greeting card.

Malcolm got off on the twelfth floor and hurried into his apartment. In the kitchen, he pitched the greeting card—unopened—into the trash. After a moment's consideration, his khakis and his Hanes followed the card. He pulled the trash bag's drawstring, tied it off, set it next to the receptacle, and replaced the bag. Then he headed for the shower, where he stayed until the hot water ran out.

Malcolm obsessed over the humiliation the rest of the evening. He supposed the fortune cookie was right. His life had changed. He was now a humorous anecdote, a laughingstock. Everywhere he went people would point and whisper and snicker. Just before he went to bed Malcolm thought of the fortune cookie in his shirt pocket.

He picked up the shirt he had been folded and placed in his dirty clothes basket. Careful not to touch the two small milk spots near the waistline, he slid the cookie out of the pocket. With no small amount of trepidation Malcolm tore open the cellophane. Uncharacteristically, he let the wrapper fall to the carpet. He cracked the cookie. The cookie joined the wrapper. Malcolm's hands shook as he opened the fortune. He flipped it over and examined the other side.

Blank. Both sides were blank.

–11–

Malcolm didn't sleep well. When he did sleep, he was visited with unsettling dreams he couldn't quite remember upon awakening. He felt certain they involved humiliation.

The following day he tried to revive his Saturday routine and managed to an extent. Though he kept to his schedule, he could not concentrate. That morning he spent two hours working on the recertification page of the National Board of Radiologists (NA BOARS). He put in the two hours, but accomplished almost nothing. His thoughts returned to the Pearsons and his own gargantuan humiliation.

His afternoon Big Ten football break included the Illinois battling his favorite team, the Iowa Hawkeyes. Though he sat with the TV on, he didn't really watch. The entire day was like that. He followed his routine as a sleepwalker might, in a dream, an altogether unhappy one.

Sunday was a little better. And Monday better still. On Tuesday he finished the NA BOARS work and moved on to the visitor's page of the California Citrus Association (CA.CA).

On Wednesday he ventured to the laundry and dry cleaners three blocks away, and then to the nearby market. No one laughed. No one stared or whispered. The orbit of his little planet had righted itself. He had moved on, returned to the routine he revered.

Except for one thing.

In those odd times when he had a free moment, when he let his guard down, his thoughts returned to Ms. Pearson and her April. Was she a widow? Had she divorced, or was April the product of an indiscretion? He wondered how they lived. She must work, and what became of April while she worked. Most vexing of all, he kept recalling Ms. Pearson's laugh, so like his mother's. What would it be like to hold her hand, to touch her face?

When he thought of Ms. Pearson's laugh, a cauldron of dormant memories bubbled forth. He had suppressed the memories of his mother, especially how her death destroyed him. He had always known his mother's importance in his life. When she died, he learned the depth and breadth of her influence. In the hollow place where her love had been, he pushed all of the anger and blame he felt as his father rebuilt the eleven year-old boy in his own image.

Malcolm was what he was, and could not change now. And he was satisfied with that. He *did* like his life.

−12−

Malcolm did not visit the Rice House that Thursday, nor the next, or the one after that. He convinced himself that he was tired of Chinese. He stuck mainly to his apartment, venturing out only for necessities.

Soon his work productivity leveled out near previous norms, and then it skyrocketed, his focus and concentration at near record highs. The odd times though, eating meals, in the shower, in bed before sleep came, his guard weakened. Those times unwanted thoughts wormed their way to the surface.

But most of the time he was just fine, even though the pizza now seemed a little soggy and *Grimm* had gone into reruns. But damn it, he liked his life.

Malcolm never believed he would see the woman and her little girl again.

–13–

The afternoon of December 21st Malcolm rode the elevator down to the lobby to fetch his mail. He hummed "Mary's Boy Child," a Christmas spiritual he had heard on the radio as he worked with CA.CA earlier that afternoon. Malcolm's mother had kept Christmas in every way, the birth, the music, Santa Claus, she loved it all.

His father abhorred the commercialization. Christmas was a time to worship the birth of the Christ—nothing else. Every Christmas while his mother lived, a cloud hung over the holiday, wet and tactile. Each parent grudgingly gave a little. Malcolm's appreciation of the spirit of Christmas included the battleground in which each parent coveted Malcolm's understanding and acceptance of their own view of the holiday. Malcolm *did* understand the concepts of both parents.

Once free of his father's influence Malcolm neither kept his mother's Christmas nor his father's. He ignored it all. Except the music. He *did* love the music.

So it was that Malcolm hummed and sang "Mary's Boy Child" as the elevator doors opened on the lobby.

–14–

A rosy-cheeked woman, all bundled up, snow melting from her boots, stood in front of the mailboxes. A scarf and hat partially obscured her face. It did not matter. Malcolm instantly knew it was Ms. Pearson. He turned back to the elevator, but the doors had closed and the indicator informed it had ascended to serve others.

Malcolm turned back to the mailboxes. Ms. Pearson stood staring. The mail slipped out of her hand and spread as if it had landed on an air hockey table. Malcolm bent to pick up the mail. Ms. Pearson bent to pick up the mail. They bonked heads. Hard. She laughed.

She did not laugh at him. Malcolm actually understood the subtlety. He understood that she laughed at the absurdity of the moment. And Malcolm wished he were capable of such laughter. Instead, he said "I'll get the mail," and he frog-walked around retrieving each piece. When he rose and gave her the mail, their hands touched. He felt none of the electricity he had imagined, though her hands did feel warm and soft.

"Mr. Blanding, I'm so glad to see you. I never got a chance to apologize for the accident in the restaurant. I am so sorry. And so is April."

Malcolm stood uncomfortably. He couldn't look at her. He looked over her shoulder and down at the faux marble floor.

"April would not stop crying. The owner came and assured us no harm was done. But we still worried about you and how upset you were."

Malcolm stared at the ribbons of color in the marble tiles. The ribbons began to undulate.

Ms. Pearson tapped the mail in her hand. "The man, Mr. Lim I believe was his name, said you came in on Thursdays. So we came the next two Thursdays. But we must have missed you."

The floor tiles churned and waved. Malcolm felt dizzy. He ended his scrutiny of the floor to find concern in Ms. Pearson's eyes.

"Oh, that's okay." Malcolm virtually whispered. "No harm done... I came to get my mail."

"You live here?" she asked.

"Yes."

"We do, too. We just moved here from Nebraska in October."

Malcolm nodded and turned to his mailbox. His throat tightened. He felt his vocal chords stretch and strain. Still Ms. Pearson did not leave. She stood right behind him. He could smell the heady mixture of her and of her perfume.

He retrieved his mail and swiveled toward the elevator. He placed one foot forward, then the other. It took maximum effort.

"Mr. Blanding?"

"Yes?" He squeaked out. Malcolm stopped, but did not turn to face her.

No matter. Ms. Pearson journeyed around him placing herself between him and the elevator. "April and I don't really know anyone in town. And each Christmas Eve I fix homemade vegetable beef soup and a spice cake to celebrate April's birthday and the coming of Christmas."

Malcolm focused on the elevator buttons just visible over her shoulder.

"Then April opens some gifts, one from me and also gifts from her grandparents and her uncle and aunt. And before bed, we read 'Twas The Night Before Christmas.' Then April and I finish by reading the Christmas story from the second chapter of Luke."

She paused and Malcolm watched her chew her lower lip.

"Would you like to join us? That is if you don't already have plans?"

Malcolm's plans, if one would call them that, were to watch National Lampoon's *Christmas Vacation*, the musical *Scrooge*, and whatever late-night Christmas fare was offered by his fifty-seven channels. Though he didn't honor or celebrate Christmas, he did like the movies—and the music.

"Uh, I'm not sure. I think I may have plans. I'll have to check my calendar." Even as Malcolm delivered the words he realized how transparent his evasion must have sounded.

Ms. Pearson chose the awkward silence to perform her own examination of the floor. Malcolm observed her. Her cheeks were rosy from the frigid wind blowing in from Lake Michigan. Most of her hair had been tucked under a stocking cap; only an outward flip on one side revealed its ash-blond hue. She was beautiful, *intimidatingly* beautiful.

"Well, we'd love to have you come if you can make it. We're in apartment 1402. Dinner's at five-thirty."

She looked him in the eyes. His tongue grew thick. "Uh, okay. I'll make it if I can, but I don't know." His voice trailed off.

She nodded. "Once again, we are so sorry about the accident the other day." She turned and pushed the up button.

"Thas okay," He mumbled.

Malcolm decided some exercise would be good. He took the stairs. For the first time ever, he walked the entire twelve flights. By the fifth floor he began to regret his decision.

–15–

Malcolm spent the next three days riding a roller coaster—a coaster of fear and excitement, of dread and anticipation. He longed to once again return to the carousel that had been his life—slow, steady, predictable circles. His precise schedule was shattered during those days, shattered and strewn about as car parts in a junk yard.

There were a few moments where he convinced himself that he would attend. Always fleeting, the exhilaration of the decision to go was overwhelmed by reasons to remain there in safety with his Christmas films.

On the morning of the 23rd, after breakfast and a shower, he noticed an envelope slid under his door.

With trepidation he opened the envelope and removed a card. The card was shiny gold with a raised white poinsettia resting on a bed of holly. Inside the card was printed *Warmly thinking of you at this beautiful season.*

Handwritten in green ink below were the words

Merry Christmas, Mr. Blanding
We hope to see you tomorrow evening
Dinner at 5:30 sharp

Jenny and April Pearson

At that very moment Malcolm knew with certainty he would not attend. And the finality of the decision left him relieved to a degree he had not thought possible. He even finished the CA.CA web pages that afternoon.

Christmas Eve brought snow in off the lake. The TV weather lady spoke of a dusting to perhaps five inches. But Malcolm didn't care. He would be inside the entire day. He worked his normal Tuesday routine through lunch. After lunch he placed a rump roast into a slow cooker, sprinkled dry onion soup mix on top along with some minced garlic. Then he spread chunks of potatoes, carrots and onions around the edges. He set the cooker on low and then read for one hour from Candice Millard's harrowing account of Theodore Roosevelt's post-presidential trip up the Amazon, *River of Doubt*.

At precisely two o'clock Malcolm set the book down on the corner of his end table and set up the DVR to play the Albert Finney musical, *Scrooge*. During the film Malcolm became distracted only once, when Ebenezer, accompanied by the ghost of Christmas past, first saw Fezziwig's daughter Belle, the woman Scrooge had loved as a young man. Though only briefly, Malcolm thought of Ms. Pearson.

After the film's uplifting ending Malcolm performed his daily fifty bent-legged sit ups and twenty pushups.

Then he made some decaffeinated coffee and exchanged *Scrooge* for the National Lampoon film.

The smell of roast wafted through his apartment as Cousin Eddie, his family and their dog Snotz showed up on the Griswold front yard. Though Malcolm identified with the film's protagonist, Clark Griswold, who only wanted an orderly, traditional, structured Christmas, he particularly enjoyed Cousin Eddie. As Eddie conversed with Clark in the snowy yard, the doorbell rang—not the Griswold's doorbell, Malcolm's.

–16–

Malcolm peeked through the door's convex peephole. He saw nothing but the wall on the other side of the hall. But the bell rang again. Immediately he thought of Scrooge's visit from Jacob Marley. Of course he dismissed the thought as illogical. He opened the door.

Below him stood April wearing a fluffy red and white Santa hat. She grabbed his hand in both of hers.

"C'mon Mr. Blandy. It's time for dinner."

The girl glowed with youthful excitement. Malcolm resisted the gentle tugging on his hand.

"C'mon Mr. Blandy. It's time for my birthday and a merry Christmas."

Malcolm looked down the hall in both directions. Leaning against the wall by the elevator stood Ms. Pearson, wearing a Santa hat and a beautiful smile. A third Santa hat dangled from her left hand.

"Please, Mr. Blandy?" The plaintiff small hand-tugging increased.

Ms. Pearson's grin widened.

Malcolm spirited his hand away from the girl.

Surprising himself, he held up one finger and said, "Wait here a minute." He left the door slightly ajar.

Inside he turned off the TV and some lights, and then moved to the kitchen. He felt goosebumps growing on his neck and shoulders. His stomach hollowed in fear and exhilaration. He lifted the slow cooker lid and took a glorious whiff of the roast before replacing the lid and switching it off. Malcolm inhaled one more giant nervous breath and exhaled.

As he closed the door, twisting the handle to make sure it was locked, he took April's hand and they walked to the elevator.

"We're so glad you could come." Ms. Pearson said. Her eyes twinkled with the irony of her words and the strong arm tactics they had employed.

"I'm coming on one condition, Ms. Pearson," Malcolm said.

Ms. Pearson's eyebrows rose.

"That you don't make me sit across the table from April."

Ms. Pearson laughed a glorious laugh. "You got it." She patted April's head and added, "Of course sitting next to her is no bargain either."

They both laughed. Yes, Malcolm laughed too. Below, April beamed up at them. They all stepped into the elevator.

"Momma, put the hat on Mr. Blandy."

"Oh, yeah. Hold still Mr. Blanding." Ms. Pearson stepped up to him, so close he could feel her breath on his neck. She placed the Santa hat on his head, cocking it slightly to the side. He felt funny wearing it—funny and embarrassed, but good.

"There." Ms. Pearson stepped back, her eyes on the hat and then on him. "Now, please call me Jenny."

"Uh...okay."

Malcolm thought of the fortune cookie and smiled.

His smile lingered, a nervous, apprehensive, glorious smile. "Merry Christmas, Jenny."

Coyote Christmas

A Fable

Darkness drew near. The coyotes crouched in anticipation on the ridge above the flock. There would be no moon tonight, and in the deep darkness they hoped the shepherds would sleep and one of the sheep would stray a bit, perhaps down to the creek for a drink. The coyotes waited. But as the sun set, something was wrong, terribly wrong.

The night sky lit up as if a huge harvest moon glowed above them. A star, the brightest they had ever seen, glowed above the town in the valley the humans called Bethlehem.

The young pup Trey looked to his parents, Tisha and Rem. Rem, rested on his haunches, stoic and unconcerned, yet Trey's mother watched the star and her mate with shock in her golden eyes.

"What can it be, my mate?" Tisha asked.

"It glows like the moon, but it is too small and the moon will hide from the earth for three more nights." Rem turned to the pup. "Young Trey, the world will surprise when you least expect it. That is why we coyotes always remain cautious. This star, if that is what it is, has never been seen by your mother or me, and it does not appear in the coyote lore passed down to us. It is, indeed, a strange omen."

Trey pawed at the ground and whimpered softly.

"Do not be afraid." Tisha nuzzled him and Trey felt better.

The star flickered from bright to impossibly bright. The shepherds below cowered among their sheep, sheep which seemed to ignore the commotion at first. But even the sheep began to display jitters, perhaps from the shepherd's behavior more than the star. Trey's father had told him that sheep were stupid creatures, which was why they were so easy to hunt when they strayed from the flock. Sheep was a delicacy that coyotes craved, and Rem's reputation as a hunter was known among animals throughout the hills around Bethlehem. Trey felt proud to be his son.

"What shall we do, Poppa?"

"Wait, my young pup. Watch and wait."

The shepherds cowered among their sheep. Trey and his mother watched Rem. He remained calm, as if it was just another night hunting field mice. Trey felt his own fear fade. Tisha crouched next to her mate and nuzzled him. Trey's father kept his eyes on the valley below.

While his poppa focused on the valley, Trey sat on his haunches in his best imitation of Poppa. He adjusted his own head to match the proud way his father carried his. Trey's father had told him about the human word *alpha*, which meant the highest rank, the first. Rem was his family's alpha. Someday, if the spirit allowed, Trey would be just like Rem and find his own mate, and love her as much as Rem loved Tisha, and he would become the alpha of his own family.

Trey's stomach growled and his mother turned to him and smiled. "Be patient, Pup."

"I am, Momma. It's only my stomach that is anxious." Both his parents smiled, though his father continued to watch the shepherds. Rem's whole family was hungry. They had only eaten a few mice during the last two nights.

Trey watched the starlight flicker in his father's eyes, and on his rust and gray muzzle. Then instantly, Rem's whole face brightened, and Trey turned to the star. It still flickered, but something small came from the star itself. It grew larger and brighter as it neared. The coyotes watched the light approach the flock of sheep.

The shepherds wailed and dug at the ground as if they were digging a den. Trey crawled closer to his father. As the glowing object neared, it took human form, only with a great bird's wings. Trey could see the night sky through this transparent human bird. The glowing human spoke to the shepherds and its soft voice carried all of the way up to top of the ridge.

The shepherds stopped trying to hide. Trey turned and saw the look of wonder in his father's eyes. The flock ceased grazing. They all watched and listened, sheep included.

Soon, many more glowing bird-humans swooped down from the sky, and all of the winged creatures howled the way humans do when they attempt to sing like coyotes. Only these voices sounded almost as beautiful as Trey's parents. When they finished their human howling they all floated up into the sky and disappeared.

Below, the shepherds jabbered on and on about what they had seen. Trey's parents looked at each other. Each look held a thousand human words and Trey felt sorry for the humans, always having always to chatter like sparrows. The look of wonder remained in his father's eyes as he shared silent thoughts with Trey's mother.

"What was that, Poppa?" Trey asked.

"We do not know. We've never seen anything like it."

"What shall we do?"

"We wait, and watch."

The shepherds ended their jabbering and all save one picked up their staffs and walked toward Bethlehem. One carried a lamb under his arm. The lone remaining shepherd sat on a boulder gazing up at the star.

"Come," Trey's father said. "We will skirt around the ridge to the brook and follow the shepherds." He trotted off behind the crest of the hill.

Tisha and Trey followed. "What if they go into the town?" Tisha asked. "Isn't that dangerous?"

"Yes, my love, it is."

"No coyote has crept near the town in many generations." she said.

Trey's father halted and Trey, right behind, bumped into him and fell down. "Tisha, I know all of that," his father said. "But I also know that we must follow the shepherds. I believe the spirit will protect us." Trey looked back and forth between them—his mother's hesitation, his father's resolve.

"Come Tisha, pup, it is what we must do." Rem loped off keeping the shepherds in sight. Trey and his mother followed.

They continued toward the town. Despite the lack of a moon, the star's glow gave a semblance of day. Trey marveled at the shadows they cast as they neared town. His own made him seem as tall as a tree. The humans entered Bethlehem and walked the lane that led to the Jerusalem side where no coyotes lived or hunted—too full of humans.

"Stay near, we keep to the shadows and small places," his father said. The shepherds were far ahead and out of sight. Only the coyotes' keen senses of smell and hearing, plus the lamb's bleating, allowed the coyotes to track them. But eventually they lost the shepherds altogether.

"What shall we do now, Poppa?" Trey sniffed air filled with strange scents. They ducked into a dark doorway as two men walked rapidly by. Trey's parents looked at each other in the darkness.

"We know where we are going, pup," Tisha said.

"But how, Momma?"

"We don't know how. A spirit may be guiding us."

Trey's father led the way as they scurried through the shadows to the far end of town. Many of the humans they passed glanced nervously at the star, but no one saw the coyotes. Trey began to feel as if his family was invisible.

His father led them around a small building. Behind stood an animal den. Its old wood seemed to glow under the full light of the star. Just inside its open doors, Trey saw the shepherds. They stood among donkeys and other animals gazing into the shabby wooden den.

"This is where we were meant to come," Rem said. Tisha nodded, but Trey wondered if they had both lost their minds. Shepherds and town humans killed coyotes when they caught them. His family would all die. Tisha stepped forward, standing next to Rem. They matched steps towards the den, their black-tipped tails swung in unison. Trey remained in the shadows. What should he do?

His father and mother stopped.

"Pup. Come," his father said.

Trey struggled with his father's command for only a moment. He might be killed if he followed. But he would surely want to die if he shamed his father. Trey hurried to catch up. At the doorway his father squeezed through the crowd, his mother nudged him along from behind and brought up the rear. Again, Trey thought of invisible-ness, as no one seemed to notice them.

Inside it smelled of fresh hay, of mold, manure and of many different human scents. Some animal ahead was screeching. The coyotes reached the front of the group and Rem sat on his haunches facing the far corner, Tisha mirrored him. Trey sat behind. Next to Trey was a human shepherd pup who kept one paw on the little lamb they had brought and another on a log with animal skin stretched across one end—not coyote skin, thank-the-spirit. The humans had many different colors of fur, and some had very long whiskers.

All eyes were turned to the corner where a new-born human pup cried in his mother's paws. The father stood above them wearing an expression of worry and of joy. Trey had never been this close to humans. Their faces showed some of the same feelings as coyotes. The poor new-born had only a tiny tuft of fur on his head and nowhere else. He must be cold. One of the humans removed a part of his colorful fur and handed it to the father, who wrapped it around the new-born.

Being wrapped in fur did not stop the pup's caterwauling though. Next to Trey, the young shepherd pulled two sticks from his fur and began to beat on the log. It was hollow and the thumping sounded pleasant. The rhythm fascinated Trey, but the new-born did not stop crying.

Without thinking, Trey began to sing. He sang along with the beat the human pup created. He howled and he yipped in his best voice. Trey's mother and father joined him. They harmonized, all to the beat of the log.

The new-born stopped crying but the human pup played on and they sang on, and soon the new-born slept. When they finished singing, the new-born's father nodded, and his mother smiled at them.

Trey's father stood and bowed to the new father. He smiled and nodded. Rem then turned to Trey and Tisha, his look saying it was time to go. As they left, the shepherds opened a path for them. Trey gave a final glance at the boy with the log. The boy grinned and Trey licked the boy's paw—it tasted salty. Then he followed his parents outside.

They took the shortest way out of Bethlehem, and once they loped clear of the roads, Rem slowed to a walk.

"Poppa?"

"Yes, pup?"

"What just happened?"

His father motioned for Trey to walk next to him. Tisha followed.

"The new human pup comes from the spirit as a gift to us all. He is their new born alpha, and not only their alpha but also their omega."

"What is omega?"

They all stopped near the peak of the hill. Tisha spoke, "Omega means the last one, the least."

Trey felt muddled. "How could he be both the leader and the last one? It doesn't make sense."

Both parents nodded. "Yes, Trey, you're right," Tisha said. "But he comes from the spirit. He will be a great leader of humans. He will teach them how to love and serve one another and how to love the spirit from whom he comes." Tisha paused for a moment, thinking. "You know how your father teaches you how to hunt?"

"Yes, Momma, he shows me how he does it."

"Exactly, the human pup will grow to be an adult and show humans how to be humble and serve others by being that way himself. He will be the alpha, but also show them that he can be the meekest, kindest omega." She cuffed Trey playfully. It felt nice. "He will change everything. And you, my brave pup, made him happy on the night of his birth."

Trey stood quietly puzzling it out in his mind. "Poppa serves us, and you do too."

"Yes, my dear pup. It's what we all should do."

"How do you and Poppa know these things about the human pup?"

His parents looked at each other. "We don't know how. We just do," they said together.

They began walking again, returning to their den. It would be daylight soon, and they had yet to stop by the olive grove to see if any olives had dropped from the trees. Trey loved olives. Then he realized something.

"Poppa?"

"Yes, pup?"

"I'm not hungry anymore. I feel as if I had just eaten the biggest meal ever."

"Yes, Trey, me too, and I have a feeling that it will last for a while."

Oh! Christmas Tree

A Mémoire

In some ways hapless Clark Griswold, Chevy Chase's character in the film *National Lampoon's Christmas Vacation*, stands as a Christmas everyman, a Bob Crachit with a holiday dose of Laurel and Hardy. Clark, a middle-class suburbanite, battles to keep Christmas as it once was, as it still should be. The poor sap loves his family's Christmas traditions and fights the good fight to uphold his ideals of the season. There's some Clark Griswold in many of us. I own more than my share. And no Christmas was it more evident than in 2004.

My desire to preserve family Christmas traditions and to create new ones developed from early childhood. I can't place an age to it, or even one seminal event. It simply happened gradually through a kind of seasonal osmosis.

Some traditions were handed down from my parents. Each year my dad brought the tree home and we decorated while Dad, after anchoring the tree and stringing lights, sat back with a martini and 'spectated.' Late each Christmas morning, we piled into the car and traveled two miles to my maternal grandparents for a Christmas brunch extravaganza and present exchange involving uncles, aunts and cousins.

Ham. My grandmother's brunch tradition included a southern-style brown sugar glazed ham so tender we didn't have to chew, but merely swish it around a bit and feel it dissolve.

My siblings—Phil and Julie—and I formed a few traditions of our own. We were not allowed to wake our parents to open gifts or even leave our bedrooms until the obscenely late hour of 6:00 a.m. Each Christmas Eve we could open only one present, any present we wished under the tree. Through trial and error our parents learned to encourage us not to open what they knew to be sweaters or socks. They nodded with knowing smiles when we laid hands on one that would keep us occupied Christmas morning while they slept to that aforementioned hour.

Well before dawn one of us—often, but not always I—woke the others. Phil and I shared a bedroom that also housed the key to survival on those interminably long pre-dawn Christmas mornings—the AM radio. These were Christmases before FM radio or in-room TVs or CDs or even 8-tracks and cassettes. Yes, we did have electricity and indoor plumbing.

Phil, Julie and I gathered in that AM-radioed bedroom, whiling away the dark hours before the Christmas dawn, with new books or board games, all the while listening to non-stop Christmas music on WHB. There are songs I still associate with those mornings, and whenever I hear them now I am zapped back to that little boy who so loved Christmas and its music. Gene Autry recalling the most famous reindeer of all, Bing Crosby's "White Christmas" to which we would whistle along with Bing at just the right time, and Mel Torme's "Christmas Song" come to mind from those Christmas mornings when the clock slowed to a snail's stroll.

My least favorite from that time, Brenda Lee's "Rocking Around the Christmas Tree," played interminably. Though my feelings about Ms. Lee's song have softened over the years, perhaps due to the memory of hanging with my sibs watching the clock's inexorable journey.

Once we rousted our parents and plied them with coffee, built a fire in our fireplace (the bailiwick of Jack-the-firebug), my sister passed out presents. We didn't take turns opening one present at a time in some kind of rotation as some families do, although we did hold off demolition until Julie had finished the sorting and

113

dissemination. Once the presents had found their new owner, we tore into them with abandon bordering on avarice. It wasn't until my teens that I discovered it can be fun watching others open their gifts.

Other traditions included my mother making a delicious breakfast featuring lots of protein and cholesterol while we kids burned wrapping paper in the fireplace. Wrapping paper burning grew into an art and a passably entertaining spectator sport. Much of what we burned, particularly the ribbon and fancy paper, delivered brilliantly colored flames and smoke. We debated the potential merits of each element waiting to be the next fire box candidate. We chanted oohs and aahs and even a few boos as the entry either exceeded or failed to live up to expectations. Sometimes my dad— who by now was armed with cigarette, a cup of coffee, and the Kansas City Times newspaper—would join in on the color commentary. It would be many years before I understood that those bright flames and colorful smoke were most likely created by toxic substances being released into the atmosphere and our living room.

The aromas that struck us as we opened the door to my grandparents' house remain with me: cigar (Roi Tan presidents) and pipe smoke (some brand that evoked cherries), that brown-sugared ham, pine scent candles, and pies. My grandmother, Mimi, created the best pies, totally from scratch using recipes passed down from her ancestors in pre-Revolutionary War Georgia. The three staples, pumpkin, mincemeat (hated it), and the best pecan pie I've ever eaten, were usually accompanied by a fruit pie of some kind. Green beans with onions and large chunks of bacon warmed in the oven, along with yams covered with a crunchy topped marshmallow crust.

Placed around the house were bowls and trays of ribbon candy, peppermints and chocolate. The grownups hung out in the kitchen smoking and drinking and chatting. Presents were not to be opened until after brunch. My siblings, cousins and I took turns shuffling to a parent and whining "When are we going to eat?"

"Soon," or "in twenty minutes," our parents lied.

Gradually the bowls and trays emptied as we darted around in that magical house, one which contained a secret room hidden next to the attic sewing room, and a dungeon that ran under the garage concealed by a wooden partition in the stone and mortar basement.

Glutted, sated, with a car full of new toys replacing the wrapped gifts for relatives, we returned home. Christmas night called for a fireplace fire and post dinner watching of Hallmark's *Amahl and the Night Visitors* (my mother's favorite) followed by the Alastair Sim version of *A Christmas Carol* in our toy strewn living room.

These memories of childhood Christmases cling tight inside, and I pull them out for viewing each Christmas. I guess that's why I choke up a little when Clark Griswold hilariously traps himself in the cold drafty attic in his empty house and dons what attic stowed clothing (women's, including a fur wrap) he can over his pajamas. Upon finding old home movies and a projector, he watches films of his childhood Christmases as the background music softens— something about old Christmases by Ray Charles—and Clark's tears flow. With each viewing I feel what Clark feels, even though I have no childhood films, because I have memories of those times, and those people, many long dead, who made Christmas so special for me.

As a husband and parent I've tried to create special Christmas traditions for my family. Nancy and I hope our children will remember them fondly even as they create new traditions for their own families. I've worked hard at it, occasionally against Griswold'ian odds.

My wife, Nancy, grew up with different Christmas traditions. We melded and compromised as we set about having children.

The Gifts: Nancy's family, having no willpower, opened all their gifts on Christmas Eve. This practice displayed the greatest gap between our family traditions, one that might have become a chasm. Christmas should be about bridging divides so, I admirably acquiesced. And for the sake of human health and world ecology we no longer burn gift wrap.

Television: There are many versions of *A Christmas Carol* out now, including Muppets, Mickey Mouse, Bill Murray, and even one with a female Scrooge. Our family latched onto the 1971 musical version *Scrooge* featuring Albert Finney. *Amahl and the Night Visitors*, as far as I know has never been shown in the color TV era, though one can still find a grizzled copy of it on YouTube. *The Christmas Story* (you'll shoot your eye out) and, of course, *National Lampoon's Christmas Vacation* have joined our family's annual list of holiday must-sees.

The Food: It varies from year to year as do the types of store-bought pies, but Nancy and I still serve a Christmas ham. These days it's store bought, spiral sliced. It comes with its own plastic-packaged brown sugar glaze. And we keep a tray of various candies on the counter in honor of those Christmases at my grandparents... and perhaps for other reasons.

The Tree: My Clark Griswold attributes leap to the forefront when it comes to the tree. In the mid-eighties, when our daughter Rebecca was still a preschooler, we took her to Candy Cane Lane Tree Farm out in the country near Harrisonville, Missouri, to cut our own tree. We, all three of us, fell in love with the practice. The country drive, the farm's festively decorated barn, hay wagon ride to the trees, the actual tree cutting, and complimentary cider and candy canes as our selection was wrapped and loaded all added to the experience. At home the pine scent lasted longer as did the time frame before needles began to drop. Never again would we purchase a pre-cut tree at a lot in town.

The following year we found a small quaint mom-and-pop tree farm near Desoto, Kansas, called Cedar Valley Farm nestled between two wooded ridges along Cedar Creek. They have all of the attributes of Candy Cane Lane and less of the mass production atmosphere and crowds.

When son Conor was born we papoosed him along as we searched. Before long Conor toddled through the trees. As he grew older we played hide and seek, and began to develop a method of selection which included agreeing on a default tree and then spreading out to look for something even better. The final decision had to be unanimous. We became discriminating and self-professed experts.

Once home, and the tree set in the corner, I string the lights. I'm ever so anal about lights. The lights must be the larger old-fashioned incandescent type—no tiny ones—and they must be multicolored. Lights well placed are attached throughout the tree's interior as well as along the outside. Even spacing is critical and clusters of like colors must be avoided. While I obsess over light placement the rest of the family unpacks ornaments. We all have our favorites, and each family member acquires a small horde of ornaments to be placed only by him or her.

These tree traditions and the untimely death of a family pet set the stage for the Kline-stamped Griswold'ian Christmas of 2004.

Our son Conor was a junior in high school in 2004. Following his kindergarten year we had gotten a puppy, the only white dog in a black Labrador show dog's litter. To the breeder's dismay, a fence jumper had visited her pride and joy show dog. We named our pup Sunshine and she unofficially became Conor's dog.

Almost twelve in the fall of 2004, Sunshine suffered from an ever-increasing list of maladies. Not long after Thanksgiving, Sunshine experienced several brief seizures and died at home—by coincidence on a day Conor was home with the last vestiges of the flu. He was with her when she died.

We live in rural Miami County, Kansas, and Conor and I buried Sunshine in our horse pasture. The solemnity of the burial gave me an idea.

Someone I knew who also lived in the country purchased a balled-and-burlapped pine each year for Christmas. After the holidays he planted it in his pasture, creating a small Christmas tree pine forest. As titular head of the household I made an executive decision.

For one year we would set aside our traditional family tree cutting trip. Instead I would purchase a balled-and-burlapped tree, as my friend did. After the holidays, we would plant the tree next to Sunshine's grave—a fitting memorial.

Two hundred twenty years earlier, almost to the day of my executive decision, Scottish poet Robert Burns anticipated said decision with his poem *To a Mouse*:

> *The best laid schemes o' mice an' men,*
> *Oft go awry,*
> *An' lea'e us nought but grief an' pain*
> *For promis'd joy!*

I didn't think of Burns' poem when I developed my live tree scheme. And at the time I considered it more as a plan, schemes having a surreptitiously negative connotation nowadays. But Burns' poem, as the best poetry does, still rings true today.

I quickly learned that in the nursery business, such trees are cut and prepped for sale during the two ideal planting seasons, September and March. Any balled and burlapped trees available in early December were leftovers. I scoured my nursery connections and those of the local municipal foresters I knew. A phone call to Rosehill nursery proved successful. They had a Scotch pine, seven-and-a-half feet tall including the ball. After work I swung by Rosehill hoping I wouldn't find an ugly duckling. I didn't. It was a fine looking tree.

"And it's got a nice big ball for successful transplanting," the nurseryman exclaimed with the pride of a natural salesman.

The price was steep, but options were absent. We sealed the deal and I told him I would drive my pickup to work the next day, Friday, and get the tree after work.

"We'll be here," he smiled.

The next evening as we settled up finances, the friendly staff at Rosehill even offered to loan me a ball dolly—a two-wheeled dolly with a round concave base—to help get the tree into the house.

I watched the first red flag rise, but refused to acknowledge it. Instead of using the loaner dolly to bring the tree to the pickup and then slide it up into the bed using the dolly's back rails, they employed a large Case uniloader with specialized forks. But then why would anyone mess with all of that hand work when the loader was available, I rationalized.

The second red flag I ignored is a bit more embarrassing now, a decade removed. When the loader deposited the tree on the truck bed, my Ford F-150 groaned audibly and its front end rose a good ten inches. The truck's front wheels barely touched the gravel surface.

On the thirty-five-mile drive home my Ford's handling felt spongy, the steering tardy and tentative. It felt as if I floated above the road, with only a casual relationship between my operation of the steering wheel and the truck's behavior.

When faced with a vexing problem I can be a fine creator of solutions. On this occasion I slowed to the speed limit. By contrast, when faced with a weighty future problem, I ignore it and hope it goes away—the Scarlett O'Hara "I'll think about it tomorrow" approach. I turned up the radio's Christmas music and concentrated on keeping my swooshing and swaying pickup on the road.

As I reached my highway exit, Elvis warned me of an impending blue—blue, blue, blue Christmas. But, on gravel at thirty-five rather than seventy, and home only a carol or two away, the pickup responded more favorably. I joined Karen Carpenter, and together we crooned a Merry Christmas, darling, Happy New Year, too. The leaden tree floated behind, miles away from my cerebrum.

I pulled onto our long gravel drive and tapped two quick horn honks. Did the truck's voice sound exhausted? Nancy and seventeen-year-old Conor met me at the house.

"Cool tree, Dad," Conor said.

My insightful wife, Nancy, also provided input. "It looks heavy."

"Substantial," I corrected. Then I provided a three-minute lecture on tree transplant survival rates and their relationship with ball size. Once planted after the holidays, our tree would survive any kind of bitter winter nature might dish out. "And the nursery loaned us their ball dolly to get it inside," I added festively.

I dropped the tailgate and explained to Conor that he and I would roll the tree ball onto the dolly and then we would slide the dolly down to the ground. Here it should be mentioned that because of my size, occupation, and sports background, I was stronger than the average fifty-five-year-old. Conor, a high school wrestler, was no slouch either. We hopped onto the truck bed.

A brief discussion of technique ensued. We positioned ourselves side-by-side on one side of the tree ball, the dolly positioned on the other side. We squatted in the proper method to avoid back strain, grabbed the bottom side of the ball and began to roll the ball.

Nothing.

The ball did not budge. We tried again, red-faced, muscles straining.

It budged. Now here might be a good place to define the word budge. *Random House Webster's unabridged dictionary* provides *"to move slightly; begin to move."* That is to say the tree did not roll onto the dolly; it merely budged.

We were down, but not defeated.

Conor and I commenced a testosterone conclave, unaware at that time of the gauntlet our tree had prepared for us. We hatched a new plan, a splendid plan. The dolly was lowered to the driveway. We spun the tree sideways. Spinning the tree in circles on the truck bed was a snap. Then with our feet anchored on the cab side we put our shoulders onto the ball and pushed as linemen push a sled in football practice. It worked. The ball was easier to slide on the slick truck bed than it was to roll. In no time—a half-hour or so— we had it to the edge of the tailgate.

Still we couldn't figure a way to get our tree on the dolly, so we accomplished the next best thing. One final herculean thrust and *thump*. The tree met the driveway. "Hello, Driveway."

Once again Conor and I palavered as Nancy voiced a laundry list of doubts and concerns. Foremost among them was that such a weighty tree might collapse the floor and end up resting on the television in the basement. We men had no time for negativity and a female's naïve logic. Soon, a new plan was born.

We closed the tailgate and rolled the dolly up against the rear bumper with the dolly's platform less than a foot from the tree ball. We tried to slide it onto the carrier, but the ball was no longer on a slick truck bed, but on rough brushed concrete. It didn't budge.

Once again Nancy voiced, "Negativity" in so many words.

Next we took the tree trunk, standing vertically since its exit from the truck bed, and began to push it downward, away from the truck. Imagine a film of the Marines raising the flag on Mount Suribachi, Iwo Jima. Then imagine the film run in reverse. In very little time, and without gargantuan effort we lowered our *flag*. We slid the dolly as far underneath the tipped over ball as possible and instructed Nancy to hold the dolly firmly in place. The Boy—I have called Conor "The Boy" since he was little as a term of endearment—and I prepared to raise our flag.

"Wait!" Nancy said, her voice rising thirty decibels.

We waited.

"What if it rolls over on top of me?"

Conor, wise beyond his years, said, "We'll raise it back off you." But his wisdom didn't stop there. "If you feel it tipping, you might want to get out of the way."

Nancy "manned" the dolly in a stance not unlike a runner waiting in the third leg of a medley relay, ready for flight the moment the baton approaches.

"On three," I said. "One, two, three!" At that very moment the Tabernacle Choir sang the Hallelujah chorus in my head, and I knew exactly how Clark Griswold felt when his outdoor lights came on. Slick as snot the ball rested on the dolly safe and snug. The Boy and I high-fived with mock explosions at the end.

The next station along our holiday gauntlet was a snap to fix. Ball dollies have wheel barrel sized pneumatic tires to make them more manageable along all kinds of terrain. Though these seemed fully aired pre-tree, they appeared flat carrying their weighty new passenger—not a problem.

Living in the country with gravel roads, a tractor and horse trailer, requires one to own an air compressor and a mobile air bubble. A few minutes later we were rolling dolly and tree toward the porch steps. The tree's weight was such that wheeling a dolly around, normally a one-man job, took two of us, but we were giddy with success.

Our home has a porch that runs the length of the house. The house is positioned on a hill, so it drops off significantly on the back side. So these two porch steps were full nine inch high steps. The steps have cedar railings on both sides preventing any attempts to lift a dolly from the sides. Nancy held the dolly in place—not that it was going anywhere—while Conor and I climbed the steps. We rolled the dolly to the base of the first step. One, two, three... lift.

The wheels never left the ground. Again the counting and again the non-lifting. I'm not sure we could have raised it with two additional high school heavyweight wrestlers simultaneously lifting from the bottom.

Rats!

When two men work a problem together, watching them discuss the pitfalls and merits of each idea can be a thing of true beauty. The same problem-solving exercise can also result in some amount of comedic value—think Abbott and Costello or any two of the Marx brothers. Our solution involved the two-ton floor jack in the garage some blocks of wood to be used as shims, a pair of removed work boots and lots of dead weight we could find. The idea was brilliant and creative. It might have worked.

While we fetched the necessary lift apparatus, Nancy remained at the base of the steps, apparently practicing her own problem solving skills. Upon our return she said, "Are you sure the ball will fit through the doorway?"

The evening breeze ceased to blow. The birds at the nearby feeder quieted. Even the new silence itself went silent. I looked at the doorway and the tree ball. My eyes ping-ponged from one to the other.

"I'll get a tape measure," Conor said.

"Shit," I said, though it was not spoken without hope. It might fit.

Conor returned with the tape measure and we measured. The tree ball was too big by at least three inches.

"Humbug," I opined. At that point I think I mentioned cutting a slice of ball off with my chain saw. But it would have been a large slice and cutting burlap, dirt, and mud will instantly dull a saw chain. An old song by Rush in which the oaks and maples were all made equal with hatchet, axe, saw popped into my head. We had all those tools, and I seriously considered them.

While I seriously considered, Nancy did too. My ideas were met with rebuttals which were firm and grounded, beginning with her default concern, "the floor will collapse" Other considerations addressed how we would water the tree ball if we couldn't lift it to slide the ball into our prearranged double-bagged trash bag container, and she mentioned issues about getting the tree back out of the house after Christmas, especially if much of the burlap wrapping used to hold the ball tightly together was no longer present.

She slid in the final dagger, "And what about your mortality rates? Won't cutting that much of the ball off mess with its chances for survival?" But she already had me at "How will you get the ball out?"

"Shit," I said, my vocabulary in a rut. I sat on the steps.

"What now?" The Boy asked.

Silence.

Unpleasant thoughts river danced in my head, the joy of Christmas a distant memory. I had already spent four times what I would have paid for a tree farm tree. So I opted for the O'Hara option. "Let's wheel this thing—it was a thing now—around the side of the house and we'll figure out something tomorrow."

The dinner table was unusually quiet that night. A fog hung around the chandelier above me. "We're not buying another tree," I said, between bites of underdone potato. The fog descended. Though the roast smelled delicious, it tasted like peppered newspaper.

I excused myself without cleaning my plate, a rarity, and went into the library to sulk. Twenty minutes later Nancy joined me.

"You in here sulking?" she said with the wisdom of Job.

I didn't want to smile. I was angry and wanted to remain so. Why wouldn't she leave me alone?

I smiled. "Yes."

"Conor and I have an idea," Nancy said. "Tomorrow you two plant Sunshine's pine and then we'll go up on the ridge and cut a cedar for this year's tree."

My head and heart were filled with misery when Nancy offered her idea and it colored my response, "That's not our property. We would be trespassing," I said with grim calm. "And it would be stealing."

She laughed. She called out to Conor in the family room, explaining what my response had been. I could hear Conor laughing, too.

An explanation of their mirth may be in order. The ridge Nancy referred to is a nearby wooded area above the tilled farmland of an absentee owner. A local farmer contract-farms the lowlands, and the woods merely sit there. We and our neighbors have ridden horses through those woods for more than a decade. And Eastern Red Cedar trees are the dandelions of the Great Plains. They pop up everywhere, useless and unwanted. Birds eat their dusty, blue berries and fly around dropping fertilizer coated seeds like German flyers dropped bombs on London. *Stealing* a cedar from that forest would be like sneaking on to a neighbor's lawn and spiriting off with a dandelion flower.

"It's a stupid idea," I said stupidly.

"Well, that's what we're doing," Nancy said. She didn't add "Case closed." She didn't need to.

The next morning I woke up with sore muscles, but in somewhat better spirits. We ate breakfast, and The Boy and I tackled the tree planting. Wheeling the 'Tree of Dashed Hopes' to its place of honor proved difficult, time consuming and energy draining. But eventually we arrived at the burial plot. Our dogs, Izzy and Quantrill, came along for support.

Another drawback to a tree with an unusually large ball, is that one must dig an unusually large hole to plant it. Shovels in hand, Conor and I commenced. Digging untilled pasture can aggravate a person who is not in the proper frame of mind. One of us was not in the proper frame of mind. One of us threw his shovel and said bad words. Unaccustomed to such a ruckus, the dogs cocked their heads, questioning, and then Quantrill returned to cleaning his penis.

There are numerous mistakes a person can make while planting a tree: leaving the burlap on will girdle roots which causes the tree to choke itself to death over a number of years. Not making the hole wider than the ball makes it tougher for roots to spread. Packing the soil too tightly, or not tightly enough, and planting the tree too high above the soil, all will make it harder for the tree to establish itself.

The absolute worst mistake one can make is to plant the tree too deeply. That's why one carefully measures the hole depth and the ball height before planting the tree. We measured the depth and the ball height carefully. The measurements were particularly tricky because we planted on a moderate incline. Once the hole was perfect we positioned the dolly at the edge and tipped it ever so gently until the tree slid into the hole.

Impossible.

The hole was too deep, and not by just a smidgeon. Short of renting heavy equipment, the tree-of-sorrow was there to stay. Conor knew little of tree planting, but he took my word that in its present circumstance our tree had been sentenced to death. Like surgeons we set to work giving it a chance to survive. First we unpinned the burlap and pushed it down to the bottom of the hole. At my parks and recreation job, we referred to this step as undressing her and giggled like school boys cutting farts.

Once she was undressed, Conor and I tried to shave the ground around the hole, which was nearly impossible in deep-rooted, virgin pasture. We dug an elaborate canal system on the downhill side to allow drainage, as otherwise the pond created would drown the tree's roots

It was hard, back-straining work, during which two shovels might have been thrown and many bad words expounded, were it not for the solemnity of the occasion. Upon completion, looking down at our handy work, with my hand on The Boy's shoulder, two things came to mind. The tree almost certainly would die within a few years, and, with exactly two weeks until Christmas I had yet to claim my annual booster shot of spirit and joy.

The gradually building anticipation of Christmas, both spiritual and secular, to which I was accustomed had taken a big self-inflicted hit. Maybe Elvis had been right about a blue-blue-blue Christmas. And maybe that's why I behaved so oddly later that afternoon.

During lunch I stuck to my empty, wrong-headed guns about the illegality and immorality of cutting down a cedar on the ridge—our plan to savagely steal a part of nature's glory from a neighbor's private property. They poked each other and chortled when I made it clear I would have no part in the heist.

Poverty Ridge—so named long ago because its rocky nature will brook no crops—rises within sight less than a half mile from our house. When Conor and Nancy prepared for their heinous theft, I couldn't keep from sticking my nose in.

"Not that one," I said, my nose stuck in. "It's too dull. Take the red-handled bow saw."

As they loaded the truck, against my wishes my mouth began to give advice about selection and cutting.

"Why don't you come along and make sure we get a good one?" my sly, trickster wife suggested.

I agreed to go for quality control only, while still vocally lambasting the caper. Nancy tossed me the keys.

"No," I said with firm resolve. "I'm not driving the getaway truck." I handed the keys to Conor. My wife and son looked at each other and tittered. I don't recall what I felt at very moment, but if I wasn't at least amused at my own behavior then I must have been in a very dark place indeed.

As we drove along 343rd to the base of the ridge, I resolved to remain in the truck and pout. Nancy and The Boy got out of the truck.

"You want to come along and make sure we get a good one?" Nancy asked.

I shook my sulking head.

"Okay," she said. "But I don't want any complaints from you about the tree we pick."

I opened the passenger door and joined the gang. Together as a family—if not quite fully in the holiday spirit—we climbed the ridge. Before we reached the woods at the summit, we found a perfect tree along the fence line. Cedars are notorious fence line interlopers. Although I gave the okay for the cut, I refused to either saw or help get the tree to the truck. Somehow my pixilated mind partitioned the benign act of accompanying and selecting a tree, from the criminal act of driving, cutting and carrying.

I want to say here that I was beginning to feel embarrassed. But, I don't remember exactly when the embarrassment stage struck. I do know that the perpetrators were having a grand time selecting and cutting our tree. And laughing at me.

Once we were safely back at the hideout I rationalized that the deed was done and I could touch the tree. Conor and I took it inside and set it up. As mentioned earlier, Kline family tradition called for me to carefully, and with great skill and acumen, install the lights. Looking at the tree, the scent of evergreen permeating, a string of woefully tangled lights dangling from my hand, the spirit of Christmas once again began to grow. I experienced what we in our family call the warm fuzzies.

One hurdle remained to be leapt over in the great tree caper of '04. If one has never been around such cedars, touched them, rubbed against their branches, it's hard to comprehend the truth of the following statement: *Eastern Red Cedar foliage tactilely might as well be made of penitentiary grade razor wire.* Though its foliage appears a pleasant green with highlights of rust, it is covered with tiny, brutal needles which scratch, puncture and slice.

A tree lighting expert, one obsessed with lighting perfection can't wear gloves—too awkward. One has to gut it out bare-handed, man versus razor-wired tree. Zip, zap, I cut my hands and wrists to shreds. Figuratively, that is, and that's how they felt though they looked merely red, scratched, and slightly swollen.

Once the lights are hung, our family tradition calls for dad to take a break while mom and the kids hang ornaments. Rebecca could not make it home for this part of our tradition, but Conor and Nancy performed admirably. My aching hands and I took a break with a glass of Irish whiskey.

From that point on the Christmas of 2004 was like many before and since, with one big exception, no Kline Christmas tree ever smelled as good, or held its scent longer than that burglarized cedar. When the family sits around the fire during the holidays swapping memories, someone inevitably brings up the "tree year," or the "year Dad lost his mind." And we laugh and tease good-naturedly before we move on to another memory.

Traditions and memories help create and rekindle the warmth of Christmas. We celebrate the birth of Jesus, who, whether one believes in him as mankind's savior or not, showed all of us how we should behave. Each December we try to practice what He preached. We are kinder, we give more and share more, and in my case, become a little less self-centered. Hatchets are buried or set aside. Families come together, if only for a brief time. Maybe some of the goodwill wears off in the cold of January. But the traditions and memories, which go back as far as we can remember, rest inside us, waiting for a spark.

A Winter Wonderland?

A Mémoire

Snow had become a four-letter word since the early nineties. Yes, the word snow *does* contain four letters, but for me snow had moved over into that category with those four-letter words that one's mother washes one's mouth out with soap for uttering. Think of Ralphie's four-letter utterance while helping Dad change a flat tire in *A Christmas Story*—Lifebuoy, I believe, was his preferred mouth-cleansing agent.

In 1993 my employer, The City of Overland Park, determined to be the #1 snow removal entity in the Kansas City metro area. To that end, our Department Heads strategically moved all Parks and Forestry employees into the Public Works winter street plowing business. We were given pagers to be worn 24 hours a day, Halloween to April 1. No, not worn on our PJs, but to be placed on our night stands. Our new *critical job function* (the Human Resources term for shanghaiing an entire segment of the workforce) dictated that we report to snow plow stations within 90 minutes of the page anytime night or day for alternating 12-hour shifts until all roads were cleared, and for me—a salaried employee—it called for no additional pay. It didn't help that I lived 29 miles from that designated plow station. It also didn't help that in order to claim Number One-ness, we had to be sitting at the ready when the first flake fell. So often we reported hours before the snow and performed herculean acts of thumb-twiddling. Several times each winter the snow missed altogether and we thumb-twiddlers got a few hours pay for the inconvenience. Except for the salaried boss-types who received only the inconvenience.

Because of my tenure and exalted boss-type rank I drew the title of Southeast Zone Snow Plow Shift Supervisor (say it fast five times) so I rarely actually plowed streets. I was there nonetheless, bossing around the plowers when they needed bossing. And I was there for the whining citizens whose freshly shoveled driveways had just been "windrowed" by a street plow, or those who claimed we've never-ever plowed their street in the six years they'd lived in *Nottingham on the Downs* (not true). I was there for the accident reports when a plow driver slid into a parked car or when a plow clipped a mailbox. There, too, for the hell-bent citizen who rear-ended one of our plow trucks and then claimed that our driver was going too slowly. I held firm and worked diligently to disarm the self-important VIP who wanted a plow to come to his house and plow him a path to work, and to be there to assist ambulances reach homes during *real* emergencies, and also to be present, sitting awake and bored at 3:39 a.m., when everything actually went smoothly. Yes, snow was a bad word.

In December of 2009, with less than a year until retirement I didn't know that we were in for the worst snow winter on record in Kansas City since they began keeping track in the 1880s. What I did know was that I had twelve days of guaranteed, off-pager leave beginning December 23rd and carrying through the New Year. I actually dreamt of a white Christmas rather than dreaded one. Here I wish to paraphrase someone famous who once said something like this sometime or another: "Watch what you're dreaming of you dummy." Along with the answer to my dreams, the next seventy-two hours would produce some exciting firsts.

On December 23rd the National Weather Service predicted rain or snow or some combination for the following day, two to four inches if it all came down as snow. Two inches would be nice, four would be perfect. Excited at the prospect, my son Conor and I took the pickup down to the south end of our property near the wood's edge. I found myself humming "Let it Snow" for the first time in two decades. We gathered firewood while our horses observed. Horses have inbred barometers and they knew better than we what approached and had worked diligently depleting the hay ring all day, stoking energy.

Christmas Eve broke cloudy with a south wind making temperatures almost comfortable. Weathermen agreed that snow and some potentially yucky stuff bore down on us. Around noon, my wife Nancy's eighty-year-old mother Bonnie arrived from Springfield. Our daughter, Rebecca rolled in soon after. We planned on an early dinner, an eight-mile drive to Louisburg for our church's Christmas Eve service, and then some heavy-duty present opening.

Just before dinner the wind shifted out of the north, and light sleet began to fall. Pellets ticked at the windows as we ate, the sound soothing from the warmth of our table. Outside, under the porch light, the sleet resembled fat raindrops until they bounced off the sidewalk like miniature ping-pong balls.

On our drive to church, the roads were fine, traction good and the sleet comically binged and bonged off our windshield and hood. We sloshed through melting sleet on pavement still warm from those earlier southerly winds, across the parking lot, across Mulberry Street and into our church. The north wind had cranked up a notch and the cold penetrated our coats and slacks.

Inside, both the temperature and the décor of our one-hundred-thirty-eight-year-old church warmed like a hot toddy with an extra shot of brandy. The hanging greens, the lighted tree and glowing stained glass gave the evening's service—the story of the lowly birth of the Christ child and the promise that birth foretold—a festive air. It added a poignant reminder of what the holiday is supposed to be about. During the hour-long service's quieter moments the howling wind outside the old building seemed as if it was designed to be a part of the service—warm and bright inside the stable framed by the cold Bethlehem night outside.

After the service, we traipsed out into a different night from the one which we experienced earlier. No more sleet, now snow thick and windblown and accumulating on the grass. As we set foot on Mulberry we found a sheet of ice had replaced the wet street we crossed an hour ago. I grabbed Bonnie and held her steady from the storm's first fist. I had never taken a frail eighty-year-old woman ice skating in dress shoes before. We yawed right. We yawed left. We slipped and slid, glided and skid. The snow, flung at thirty mph, stung our eyes, but somehow we baby-step slid across the street and through the lot to the car. Our family arrived at the car with only one minor mishap. Conor, our twenty-two-year-old son, decided the conditions were ripe for competitive long-distance sliding. Conor neared a Louisburg town distance record when his feet outpaced the rest of him and he finished the slide on his derriere, which according to town distance sliding rules disqualified him. But his butt and bones took the fall with youthful grace.

The drive home was treacherous, the traction nearly non-existent. Snow had not yet accumulated on the road as its icy surface was too slick to capture it. So we rolled home on a sheet of ice. Our headlights struggled to penetrate the darkness, and the blowing snow made it difficult to even see the road. Fluctuating waves of low-blown snow covered the road's surface like some eerie swirling fog, a fog that might at any moment produce Jacob Marley, tire-chains and all. With no traction we would surely run over him, or through him, depending on how apparitions operate.

The wind buffeted my wife, Nancy's candy-apple red P.T. Cruiser. It blew so hard that it seemed as if no snow actually fell, but rather merely blew across Kansas on its way from Nebraska, where it had originally fallen, to its final destination in Arkansas. But once we reached home safely we found ample evidence that much of the blowing snow was here to stay.

Our house sits well back from the road and is accessed by a three-hundred-foot-long gravel drive that undulates across uneven terrain. Though snow had begun only an hour earlier, it already drifted in the drive's nooks and crannies. We easily poofed through the feather-light mounds and pulled into the garage.

Conor and I fetched firewood from the side of the house and built a fire. The wind outside ramped up. We heard its ferocity and watched snow blow and swirl outside. Once settled around the fire we matched the wind's ferocity as we opened presents, paper flying and falling like plump colorful snowflakes. Christmas carols on the stereo struggled to overcome the outside wind's clamor.

After presents were discovered and cooed over, and those sugar plum visions no longer danced, as our bellies were assuaged with empty but tasty calories, we turned on the late news, which advised us that our home stood in the center of a blizzard warning, the area's first since 1982. Following that chilling news, we successfully viewed National Lampoon's *Christmas Vacation* ("Are you serious, Clark?"), and then we all settled down for a long winter's nap.

We don't have a storm door on our west-facing front entrance because we have a long wide porch with a roof overhang, and well, we just didn't want one. We keep a "door sock" along the threshold to protect against drafts in the winter. Still, our relatively new house with double-pane insulated windows and other modern weatherproofing felt drafty as sleep overtook us. While we slept, the storm raged.

An early riser, I was the first up Christmas morning. I rose to discover the burgundy-colored door sock covered with a fine white powder, no not powder but powdery snow that had blown under the eaves, across the porch and insinuated itself between the door bottom weatherstrip and the threshold. There was also a little puddle around the sock that looked as if our dog Whitey had lifted his leg and peed on it, but it wasn't yellow and though Whitey lifts his leg on nearly everything outdoors he does have a modicum of couth indoors.

I cleaned up the mess, stuffed the door sock back against the threshold, tossed a throw-rug on top and then began to fry sausage for biscuits and gravy. But not before I put on a pot of coffee.

Coffee. I managed to avoid the addictions that afflict most addicts: drugs, alcohol, cigarettes, snuff, chew, prescription meds, but I couldn't escape the nefarious clutches of coffee. I managed to avoid it up until the summer of my twenty-first birthday. That summer I took an automobile trip to the west coast with my coffee-drinking chums Dan Lorch and Lynn Lippoldt. I left Lawrence an innocent, and returned a coffeoholic. I'll never forgive Dan and Lynn, never.

Apparently Bonnie smelled the sausage—or more likely the coffee—and wandered in, opened the cupboard and clutched a cup. Our kitchen sits next to our dining area which has floor to ceiling windows facing south and east. With the sun just peeking over the east woods we marveled at the amount of snow, and the size of some of the drifts. It still snowed lightly from above, but near the ground the wind continued to rearrange the snow's final resting places making it appear to be a blizzard along the surface. I wasn't sure if I had ever seen this much snow fall in twelve hours, possibly excepting the Colorado mountain ski-bum days of my youth. Bonnie and I sipped coffee while I turned sausage and did the prep work for gravy and biscuits. We spouted snow-storm platitudes.

"I remember the blizzard of thirty-nine," she parried.

"Before my time," I answered.

"This is *at least* as much snow as we ever got overnight in Steamboat back in 76," I thrusted.

136

We continued our figurative blade-dance back and forth, with one-up blizzardy half-truths until I heard stirrings from above.

"Sounds like the kids are up," I said. They were. A few minutes later I could hear Rebecca clumping down the stairs. I could tell that it was her: Rebecca clumps, and like his father, Conor stomps.

Neither of my kids had yet succumbed to the wiles of coffee so she didn't instantly reach for the cup cupboard. Instead, she offered me a worried look. "Dad, I need to show you something." I returned her look with my version of the *uh oh* face. First, I turned the temperature way down on the sausage and then followed where she led, which was up the stairs.

Now, in order to properly set up what came next, we must discuss roofs and roofing materials. Bear with me.

When we built the house, we chose a forest-green standing seam metal roof. They are more fire-resistant, last longer and, to our eyes, are more attractive than the materials used around here. They are the rage in heavy snow areas of the mountains because snow doesn't continue to collect on them but rather collects to a modest amount and then slides off. The seams run vertically so it doesn't impede snow slides but enhances them. Another advantageous feature of the design is its metal ridge cap. Standard roof's ridge caps fit snugly on the top row of shingles. These roofs need those sheet metal rectangles and round turbines to allow the attic's heat to escape, so it doesn't build up to a stifling degree that defeats cooling the house in summer.

The metal ridge fits along the edge of the roof's seams, not flush on the base metal, leaving a series of one-inch-high gaps between the seams. These seams are filled with attached inserts that are pocked with tiny pushpin-head-sized holes to allow all of that hot air to escape, thus no need for sheet metal turbines or any other roof venting. Tah-dah, another plus for standing seam. But remember that Greek guy Achilles and his heel—the one mortal spot on an otherwise immortal being? It seems those seams and the ridge cap are a standing seam's Achilles heel.

Just as Paris' arrow found Achilles' heel, a dry, fluffy, light-weight snowfall combined with gale-force winds (45-51 mph according to the National Weather Service) blowing from just the right direction blew snow *up* our roof, under the ridge cap and through those pushpin holes.

"Look, Dad, look at the ceiling at the top of the stairs."

What I saw was a wet stripe that ran down the hall from Rebecca's door to Conor's.

"It's inside my room, too," Rebecca said.

Conor's door opened. "And mine."

Shit.

I grabbed a flashlight and the stepladder. The entrance to our attic is a tiny square on the ceiling of Rebecca's crowded closet. I tossed my robe on her bed and climbed the ladder in sweats and a Parks and Rec. t-shirt. I pushed open the door and poked my head into the cold, dark attic. A quick swing of the flashlight told me what I needed to know, what I should have guessed but did not. Inside the attic there was a foot-high, eighteen-inch wide mound of snow that ran directly under the roof's ridge-line the entire length of the house. It had begun to melt.

Nancy's extra-long winter's nap had concluded by then and the family huddled in the kitchen. The plan called for the girls to finish fixing breakfast while the boys accomplished a second exciting first: shoveling snow in the attic on Christmas Day. That feat may not have been *solely* a Kline family first by the way; a roofer friend told me later that he had never heard of it happening, even in the mountains—a perfect storm if you will. How all of that snow squeezed through those tiny holes remains a Christmas miracle.

The job of shoveling snow in one's attic presents some logistical challenges. Shovel snow to where? With what? As it turned out our super, extra heavy-duty Ace Hardware snow shovel wouldn't fit through the opening. And what does one wear when shoveling snow indoors (technically indoors anyway)?

As Southeast Zone Snow Plow Shift Supervisor (say it fast five times), logistics were my bailiwick. Conor and I logisticized. We selected a long-handled flat scoop shovel and a roll of those giant yellow fundraiser trash bags. Having been up there before working on the attic fan I recalled that there is no floor up there and we would be required to step from two-inch thick joist to joist. If we slipped and stepped in-between them, down through the ceiling we would come in a flash. So Conor in his pajamas and I in my sweats, both in bathrobes, donned our sturdy joist-stepping boots.

Once we climbed into the attic we discovered two additional challenges. #1. We are both over 6' tall which would require us to stoop at all times—not so bad for a 22 year-old back, but mine had significantly more mileage. #2. Our attic insulation was not only very thick, but was not the roll variety. In the dim light of the sole 60-Watt bulb and my puny dying-battery powered flashlight our attic looked like a field of giant pink cotton balls, and it was deep enough that it obscured those joists we were required to keep our feet on—sort of like walking a minefield. Oh yeah, it was bitterly cold up there.

We filled the first bag with snow and pink insulation in no time, but it was too heavy to lift. So I emptied about a third into a second bag to make it manageable. We called for reinforcements as this would take many bags. We filled and handed them down to Rebecca who took them onto the deck that was so laden with drifted snow that she struggled to get the door open. Rebecca then dumped snow and giant, pink cotton-ballish insulation over the edge of the deck onto the ground below. No matter how much fun this sounds, it wasn't that fun at all.

Before you could recite the Night Before Christmas one thousand times we were done, and done in. Our hands stung as they thawed at the breakfast table. In less than an hour we had fully recovered and once again glowed with Christmas spirit (no not spirits, it was breakfast time, silly). We ate our biscuits and all had a good laugh. The Boy and I even considered beginning our own door-to-door attic shoveling business now that we had the hang of it. One minor detail that none of us considered was left that way, unconsidered. We have two roofs and two attics, one over the house and one over the garage.

After breakfast we took a good look outside at the havoc wreaked by the night's storm. It was bad. It was beautiful. We have a place on our deck where northwesterly winds never reach, and in that drift-free location our yardstick measured 14". Our horses stood at the hay ring with a coat of white on their backs, as if they each wore a fluffy white blanket.

It still snowed lightly and the wind still blew fiercely. Don Harmon and the rest of the local television news gang informed us that accumulations were at an end, but they added the codicil that temperatures were in single digits and expected to remain that way for the next thirty-six hours. Wind chills hovered well below zero and our blizzard warning had transitioned into a frostbite warning.

Rebecca was due for Christmas day dinner at her boyfriend's in Leavenworth, and Conor at his girlfriend's in Leawood. No problem. If the tractor would start, we could blade away the waist-deep drifts in our extra-long driveway. There would also be the minor hurdle of the gravel road that we live on being nearly three miles from any paved road of significance. Rural Miami county did not have the commitment or resources to rival Overland Park. We would have to wait for the county grader to clear the heavily drifted road before the kids could strike out for points north. And we were a ways down on the priority list. And it was Christmas Day.

The kids and I bundled up and went outside. Bitter cold. The electric stock tank heater could not keep the horses' water tank ice free as it normally did. Instead, it concentrated on keeping a small hole open, just large enough for them to get a drink—smart heater, that. Wind had distributed snow haphazardly. Places, including portions of our 300' driveway, looked as if we had only gotten a light dusting. Within a few feet of such spots stood drifts in which you could lose a yardstick. It was frostbite cold.

As a lark, I tried to start the tractor. The ancient Ford chuckled once and was silent, not even a tell-tale dead battery clicking. But it really didn't matter unless the County grader arrived to clear Rockville Road. I did, however, run an extension cord to the Ford and attached a battery charger.

The sun came out briefly during Christmas Day, which caused huge snow-slides off our roof. They were pleasant to watch and produced some really special sounds as they slid off, thunking onto the drifts below. The wind still blew strong, rearranging the snowfall's mountains and valleys, and the county grader never made it down our street. We spent the day around the fire playing games, working on a thousand-piece puzzle, stoking the fire and watching *The Bishop's Wife* and of course *A Christmas Story*. Once again, only Ralph's glasses saved him from shooting his eye out.

Phone calls to those north of us expecting our kids revealed that things were a mess everywhere. The Kansas City area experienced 10-12 inches. On the evening news our weatherman pal Gary Lezak informed that a few scattered flakes may linger, but the major storm was on its way to the Great Lakes. Gary did warn that wind chills would remain below zero for the next 36 hours.

We also ate. We ate pies—turkey, ham, Aunt Lee's cinnamon popcorn balls, crackers and a port cheese ball, shell-yourself mixed nuts. We swilled a collection of Christmas ales fetched from a south-KC mega liquor store. It was a grand white Christmas, complete with howling wind noises that were so authentic they sounded fake.

Our dogs, who like the outdoors and who enjoy gallivanting in snow, only ventured out long enough to handle their bodily functions and then hurried back. Mostly they lay around the fireplace sleeping. Occasionally, Quantrill our old black–lab mix, rolled over on his back spread-eagled, showing off his neutered privates. Bonnie, who was not used to Quantrill's R-rated exhibitions, commented on our pet's overall lack of couth. We offered to allow him to return with her to Springfield and she could teach the old dog new tricks about proper decorum. She declined.

Before nine the following morning the county's grader rumbled up our road, rolling the massive drifts off to the west side of Rockville. That left only the three hundred feet long driveway between us and getting our kids to their belated obligations. I already mentioned that there were long stretches that appeared to have already been shoveled, due to the wayward wind's whims. There were other long stretches that appeared much like what I would imagine one would see in central Antarctica.

I made a quick visit to the tractor, dang it was cold out. The tractor agreed. She voiced three brief rurs and then went back to sleep. I hurried inside.

While we donned *A Christmas Story's* Randy-the-slug-like layers of warm clothing, our local weather warned not only of the frostbite warning still in effect, but provided a public service segment including an interview with a gerontologist stating that old people who shovel snow in such weather greatly increase their risk of heart attack. I didn't feel like "old people" but as I turned sixty that year, I had transitioned into a newly installed old person. Our federal government officially recognizes the onset of old person-ism at sixty-five, as that's when they kick in Medicare and full Social Security benefits. But for some time, sixty had been inked as a cultural tattoo, reading *old. He's old; he's sixty.*

As we waddled out in our multiple layers, Conor voiced his concern over my heart and urged me to take-it-easy. We went directly for the most gargantuan drift, about one hundred feet from the road where the drive rolls through a swale. I don't believe that I had ever shoveled snow that deep, not even in my days as a Colorado western slope ski bum. The good news: the snow was incredibly light and fluffy. The bad news: the snow was incredibly light and fluffy and it swirled in the wind as we flung it, some of it inevitably flying back in what little bare facial skin we had. And we had to throw it only to one side (south) of the drive or wind would instantly return to its familiar spot.

After only a few minutes, Conor suggested I go back inside.

"I was out shoveling in more snow than this before you were born, whippersnapper," I informed.

"I know, Dad, that's what I'm saying. You're an old fart now."

That frosted me. I determined that I would shovel as long and as hard as he did or keel over with a heart attack trying. It became readily apparent that maybe I could shovel as long as he, but no way nearly as hard. He shoveled like someone might in those old cartoons, where his arms and shovel were a blur and all that one could see was the snow flying, as if he held some incredibly silent snow blower. I, on the other hand, shoveled more conservatively as befits an old fart. And I took frequent but brief rests.

By the time we tunneled through the two worst drifts, we had gone from warm to sweaty to wet to clammy to cold. We went inside. Nancy, who saw the same TV news piece on old-timer heart attacks, called our neighbor Paul who had a four-wheel-drive pick-up. We did not have one, but this would be our last winter without one I swore.

Paul, who is a veterinarian in nearby Drexel, and who had made it in to work swung by on his way home for lunch and ran up and down our driveway, pounding the smaller drifts into flat tracks. Rebecca left shortly after in her late-model Buick. She slid around the drive a bit, but successfully navigated it and headed south on Rockville. North is the quickest way to get back to the city, but the farmhouse grapevine reported that the intersection a mile north at 335th was impassable, that the grader could not move enough snow. Turns out they were correct and on the 27th it would take the county loader several hours to dig it out.

Now Conor had a 1983 Oldsmobile. It was rear wheel drive. We old people recall the days when all cars were rear wheel and we recall how they performed in snow—abysmally. So we loaned him Nancy's old PT Cruiser, which was front wheel drive. PT Cruisers, it turns out, also have Achilles heels. Part of their sleek design dictates that they appear to be low-riders. The way Chrysler designed that low-rider appearance was, well, to design them to ride low.

Conor shot right through the areas he and I had shoveled, but bottomed out in a drift where Paul had merely flattened the way for tires. The Cruiser's wheels spun mightily, but it was high centered on a mountain of snow.

We bundled up again and went to work on the Cruiser. Let's see if we can list the *firsts*: the first time ever that this old man and his son shoveled a driveway as long as a football field; the first time we did so during a frostbite warning; and it was the first time we

144

ever shoveled snow out from under a car, watching its wheels slowly sink as we removed the snow holding its body off the ground.

Once we got the car free, we spiffed up the drive's remaining thirty feet. Conor ran inside and shed his Randy-the-slug garments, hopped back in the Cruiser and he was on his way. He didn't get far.

Before I could discard my slugware we received a call. Conor had made it a mile or so down to the Drexel road intersection where he slid into a ditch. I was miffed.

As a kid my whole family watched a TV show called *Father Knows Best.* Robert Young played the calm, cool, collected father who almost always did know best. The kids, Betty, Bud and "Kitten," always seemed to get into scrapes and Dad, with grace and aplomb helped extract them while teaching his kids valuable life lessons. I'm leaving the mom, Jane Wyatt, out; I don't know why, probably something Freudian. Anyway, I have tried to be like that calm man on TV who always knew best, with occasional success.

My twenty-two-year-old son obviously drove too fast for conditions. I remembered when I was that age: brash, impetuous overconfident. At that age I believed that I was a superb driver, superb at most things actually. The apple didn't fall far, and I could just see my boy flying down the road, planning to power-slide that turn. I would teach him a life lesson about driving with care on bad roads. I hopped in my stick shift Cavalier and took off. The driveway was difficult to manage and the stick came in handy—nothing like a front-wheel drive manual transmission for driving in snow, unless of course it was the four-wheel drive pick-up I had been meaning to get for several years.

On the road I discovered two things, the snow had been bladed off but on the wings of the wind it had begun to return, and also that with the snow bladed off, the road was back to the layer of ice from melting sleet and from freezing rain Christmas Eve. No matter, the prudent driver slows down. I did. From several hundred feet away I saw that the Cruiser was not likely to be pushed out by mere mortals, even with the shovels I had on board.

I slowed to a crawl as I neared the intersection and lightly applied the brakes—nothing. I pumped the brakes and still nothing the car slowed, not from braking but from the inertia caused by ceased acceleration. My, it was slick. The Cavalier stopped in the intersection. I carefully backed, retreating onto our road. The life lesson I had rehearsed had already retreated into my cranial dead-letter file. But as if to add emphasis, the second that I stepped out of the car both of my feet reached for the sky and I landed hard on my rear, elbow and pride. The dead-letter file closed with a resounding boom. I must say that my buttocks wore the technicolor of that mishap for weeks.

Conor stood by his ditched car displaying proper concern; after all, I was an old-person, a walking heart-attack. Before calling for help we performed some shoveling and pushing and found that the Cruiser could go back and forth in the ditch quite a ways, but not climb out. I called our local rural tow service, Cutshaw Tow. By now we were on a first name basis with both the dispatcher and the drivers—a perk of living in the country and owning a bevy of vehicles over ten years old. We were in luck, even though this nightmare storm had created a backlog of potential towees, our favorite driver was just finishing a highway median extraction a mile away. He would take care of us before heading north for his next call.

While we waited, Conor and I had a few chuckles, examined my war wounds, the knot on my elbow and the already colorful spot where hip meets left buttock. Lectures were neither delivered nor deserved, and the father only *thought* he knew.

The Cutshaw driver, our favorite, was a hoot. He was giddy from lack of sleep and visions of overtime dollar signs dancing in head. We all had fun pulling the Cruiser out while he told us stories of the havoc wreaked on the roads and highways around us. The Cruiser out, and me out $110, Conor carefully crept away to the city.

Once I returned, I found that Rebecca had phoned. She had made it to her destination in Leavenworth. She, too, told Nancy tales of winter wonderland, with cars strewn like tree ornaments.

We had one more trip to make. Nancy and I had to drive to White's Automotive (yes, their real name, not just some writer's cheap word trick) to pick up her car that had been in the shop for brake work. Suffice it to say, it was a white-knuckles (now that white *was* a writer's cheap trick) drive all the way, to White's and back home... for both of us.

All of my life I have eagerly dreamed of having a white Christmas here in the heart of America. There have only been two or three that were true white Christmases and not solely one where a few patches of a previous storm had not completely melted. Christmas of 2009 made up for all of those clammy forty-five degree ones. It was one that all of us who experienced will not soon forget. The snow still covered the ground five unseasonably frigid weeks later.

When it did finally warm up some, we were reminded of that second roof, the one over the unheated garage. Our reminder occurred when the melted-snow, water soaked, sheetrock garage ceiling collapsed on top of Nancy's car. The snow melt outdoors also revealed a large pile of giant pink cotton ball chunks of insulation next to the deck where Rebecca had dumped those bags of attic snow. It looked like a mountain of cotton candy.

So what did I learn? Christmas is Christmas no matter what the weather. We would do well to remember what we celebrate. I re-learned that my family enjoys being together, no matter what wacky challenges we face. My love for my family remains strong whether sipping coffee by the fire, shoveling waist-deep snow or pushing a car back and forth in a ditch.

One thing I *DO* wonder—other than we Klines, is there anyone else out there, living or dead, who has ever shoveled snow in their attic on Christmas morning?

The Fiftieth

Dedicated to Bill Myers and the memory of his Faye

He sits on the window seat in the front room watching it snow. Wind, which so commonly accompanies such storms, has taken a vacation on this December afternoon. Plump flakes float lazily downward as if they have all day to reach their destinations—which the weatherman confirms they do. The storm will continue into the night. Laura would have called it a Hallmark Channel snow.

If only she were here beside him. Laura so loved snow. Tomorrow would have been a milestone, their fiftieth Christmas together, but instead it marks his third without her.

Despite the heavy cabled-sweater he feels a chill by the window. The fireplace, which held blazing fires so often on Christmas, stands cold and barren. Laura loved the fire's warmth and beauty. And he was delighted to build them and tend them and bask in the glow of his creation and in the special glow on her face as she watched the fire flicker. Now the effort and the memory are more than he wants to take on.

Laura loved a warm, toasty house. Too warm. He liked it cool. As young newlyweds learning to live together—the give and the take required—they fought thermostat wars, not angry wars, but wars of loving deceit and laughter. Long ago he gave in—he always gave in—and learned to live in a toaster. Now the old house is the way he likes it, cool, a scant comfort measured against loss of the most important part of his life.

In the front yard, cardinals and blue jays and more modestly adorned birds dig in the snow for the black sunflower seeds he sprinkled as he picked up the paper that morning. Those footsteps now rapidly fill with fluffy flakes. He can almost feel her lean her head on his shoulder as he watches the scene.

"Isn't it beautiful," she would say. And he would kiss her forehead and nod. Then her head might pop up as she sits upright. "We should get a photo of the snow and the birds and your big footprints for next year's Christmas cards!" They would both laugh. He does have big feet, much bigger than his slender, bony body had a right to drag around. God, he misses her.

God?

Though they went to church every week, and though Laura was a devout believer, he always had doubts. His faith faltered, smaller than a mustard seed. Laura's death confounded him. How could he believe in a loving God who would take her away? Still, he harbors hope that there is such a being, and there is such a place as heaven where they will someday reunite. But it is hope. Not faith. If he knew she waits there, he would join her tonight.

If the snowplows trek out tonight, Ted will come and pick him up in the morning for Christmas Day with him and Alice at their place. He will celebrate with his son, Ted, and Ted's family, complete with grandkids and his new great-grandson. The red and white sacks of presents from Target wait by the front door. In past years, on Christmas Eve this house would be filled with the aroma of cinnamon, pumpkin, and spices as Laura baked pies for Ted's family celebration—two pumpkins, one pecan, and one mincemeat. No one living made better pies than Laura. He smiles at the memory. How seldom he smiles these days.

His heart is no longer into decorating the house for the holidays. He used to enjoy the chore because it made Laura so happy. And that first lonely year he did follow through, enduring the pain and tears. And then he battled more pain, and more tears repacking the decorations afterward. Since then, he only unpacks the eighteen-inch table-top tree, complete with plastic fruit and wild birds they got from the National Wildlife Federation. He places it on the breakfast table. Even so, every morning and every evening the tree stands as a bittersweet reminder of happier Christmases.

***

That night, the night before Christmas, all is quiet as he eats his Campbell's Chicken Noodle soup at the table with the tree. Christmas music used to permeate the house—music from the radio and albums, and later from CDs, and still later from myriad Sirius Christmas channels. They had so many yuletide songs they loved. Now he has only songs to avoid. Will he ever reach a point where the pain of hearing the music ends and the song's memories become sweet and worthwhile?

As he eats, he hears the snowplow's metal blades grinding on snowy asphalt. There would be a Christmas celebration at Ted's tomorrow. He will buck up and make merry with his family.

He does stay up to watch *The Bishop's Wife* on television before he goes to bed. The film was one of their favorite Christmas movies. Cary Grant plays an angel brought to earth by the Christmas prayer of a bishop in a moment of doubt.

They would have snuggled on the couch in their fire-warmed toaster of a house all decked out in the glory of the season. They would watch arm-in-arm, and laugh and cry at all of the right places. Instead he sits alone, chilly though wrapped in a blanket, watching it play out, staunching tears.

At his bedside he kneels to pray. He doesn't remember the last time he prayed. He prays to Jesus, the birthday boy. He prays that Jesus be the real thing, that his promise of life after death be a good promise, that one day Jesus will reunite him with his Laura.

Often, he lies awake for some time, replaying his life, their life together. On this Christmas Eve he sleeps easily.

Sometime in the night he hears a voice.
"James, James."
He often dreams about Laura.
"James, it is time."
He took her hand.

Brady Kirby's Christmas Story

Brady Kirby had a problem. He couldn't write. It wasn't that he couldn't write at all, he still cranked out bestseller after bestseller. Horror was his genre. His problem grew from an uncharacteristic obsession to write a Christmas story each of the last eight years. And each year after that first one Kirby put it off until time grew short, until he felt himself under the gun. Writing Christmas stories with an imaginary gun held to one's head was not conducive to quality holiday literature. But once Christmas loomed near, he always managed to cobble something together.

His agent, Ned Scanlon, said the stories were good. Ned had even sold a few. But why did Kirby even bother when it was such a big hassle, if every year he worried and fretted as the twenty-fifth slunk toward him? And Kirby didn't need the spare change the sale of his stories brought. So why?

It all began with the coyotes.

Something changed him that Christmas of the coyotes eight years ago. That Christmas—four years after his divorce—he planned to spend the week writing the latest novel in his secluded woodland home about an hour south of Kansas City. Also that year, same as the previous three, his ex-wife, Tanya, invited him to Christmas Day dinner with their grown kids. But each year he passed on the invite and had his publicist send gifts to the kids. Kirby believed his horror writing was strongest at Christmastime, and he was certain that his writing was most prolific. He didn't need frivolous interruptions. Until that year of the coyotes he had never written a Christmas story, never even considered it.

But eight years ago they turned Christmas topsy-turvy. Living out in the country in heavily wooded Miami County, Kansas, had benefits for a writer such as Kirby. He thrived on solitude. His place had it in spades once Tanya left. One intrusion he enjoyed was coyotes howling from the woods behind his house. He'd heard them, and discovered their tracks along the creek in the mud and snow, but he'd rarely actually seen them until two days before Christmas.

Rousted by an uncharacteristic racket he found a male coyote caught in a steel leg-hold trap. The coyote had dragged the trap onto Kirby's property near the creek. The coyote—and others, it appeared—had tried to gnaw his leg free, tearing up his leg and paw further. Kirby attempted to pry open the trap without success. Initially deciding to leave the coyote to live or die, to let nature take its course, Kirby had returned home.

Once home he couldn't write. He couldn't exorcise images of the coyote and his pals chewing off his leg to free him. Fearing the coyotes would attack him upon his return, Kirby brought a gun when he retrieved the injured coyote. He bound it and the trap in a bedspread, making it immobile and unable to bite, then carried it inside his home. Though they didn't attack, the coyotes followed him and waited at the edge of the woods. One coyote—the trapped one's mate, Kirby guessed—paced in the yard.

On the internet Kirby researched how to open the trap and popped it open. But the animal was in bad shape. He nursed it as much as he was able, and as he went to bed on Christmas Eve the coyote lay on the floor of his library, bandaged, medicated and panting harshly. Kirby expected to find it dead on Christmas morning. As he prepared to climb the stairs to his bedroom, a cluster of coyotes at the edge of the woods watched him through the library window.

After a series of wild dreams, Kirby had awakened to a great racket in the house below. Grabbing a baseball bat, he crept down the stairs. The bandaged coyote, apparently recovered from its injury, was tearing through the house smashing up furniture trying to find a way out. The other coyotes threw themselves against the back door as if trying to knock it down.

With little thought about what terrible outcome might befall him, and treading barefoot across broken window glass, Kirby opened the door. His coyote tore past him, cavorting joyously into the backyard. The coyotes did not attack. They danced in the snow, spinning circles as if they chased their own tails. After a few moments they ran deep into the woods—all except one.

The coyote Kirby took to be the trapped one's mate stood at the edge of the clearing. That day Kirby was positive she made eye contact with him, and nodded before following the rest deep into the woods. That's the way Kirby told the story, anyway. As each year passed, he became less sure of the eye contact and the nod. It sounded too much like a storyteller's flourish, like literary license.

On that Christmas morning eight years ago, after bandaging his feet and slugging down four fingers of bourbon, Kirby called Tanya and accepted the dinner invitation. When he had returned home that Christmas night after dinner, he felt as if he had dreamed the whole coyote thing—that is until he opened the front door and gazed upon the destruction inside. He turned on the back lights and peered out the kitchen window. The backyard was covered with paw prints.

Kirby booted up his PC and began to write the story, his first Christmas story. Whenever Kirby wrote he allowed his imagination free rein to play tricks on him, as a part of his writing process. His horror stories featured all manners of demons and evildoers cohabiting his library as he tapped out the pages. His characters, both good ones and bad were in the room with him as he wrote. He wasn't off his rocker. Kirby invented them and they came to life as he wrote. And then they disappeared as he closed up his literary shop for the day. At a book reading and signing in Denver once, someone asked him if he ever had nightmares.

"Never," he said casting forth a tiny white lie. "When I shut off my computer my characters go back where they came from. And then I deadbolt the door." The large crowd laughed heartily, which was his intent.

That night eight years ago as he wrote his first Christmas story, Kirby felt—no actually saw—his coyote perched next him, on its haunches, looking over his shoulder watching what he wrote. The coyote no longer panted in pain, but behaved more like anyone's healthy pet dog. And each time Kirby paused to stretch, he saw the coyote's mate outside, her wet black nose smudged against the glass.

For the next seven years Kirby had written his Christmas stories, and when he went to Christmas dinner with Tanya and the kids he brought them each a copy. The story, as much as anything else, helped him repair some of his failure as a husband and father.

Once again, it was Christmas Eve Eve, as his mother used to label December twenty-third. Kirby was flummoxed, stricken with writer's block. For the ninth time he closed his eyes and waited for inspiration.

"What about another Santa Claus story?"

Kirby's eyes snapped open. In the recliner facing the fireplace sat a rotund man in a red jacket. The fire burned brighter when only a moment earlier he thought about bringing in more logs to replenish the fading blaze. Though the man faced away from him, gazing into the fire, Kirby knew him. He recognized the voice. The man was Kirby's Claus.

"Sorry, Santa. The two Santa stories I've already written have pretty much tapped me out. No offense."

Kirby's Claus held an abnormally large meerschaum pipe. The smoke that curled off into the fireplace smelled of cherries. "None taken," he said in between puffs.

156

"That is, unless you've got a great idea you want to share?" Kirby said.

Santa's laugh held perfection. Maybe not for other people, for it contained no hint of ho, ho. But for Kirby the laugh was quintessential holiday stuff. Santa's laugh dwindled. "You're the writer, young man. Write what you will of me... just as long as there are no witches or devils or axes chopping up body parts."

It was Kirby's turn to laugh—not an imitation Santa laugh, but his own genuine one. "Wouldn't do that to you, old fella. Might get thorns and ashes in my stocking."

Another perfect laugh. "After fifty-six years the boy's finally catching on."

Kirby grinned. "Thanks, Santa, but I'm thinking I won't be writing about you this year."

"So be it." Santa touched the side of his nose and faded away up the chimney in a blizzard of cherry-scented smoke.

"What about us? You've never written exclusively about us," said the pushy elf in one of Kirby's Santa stories.

Six male elves in garish, Kelly green and yellow jackets over forest green yoga tights stood in the library entrance. Kirby couldn't remember the name he'd given the cocky one who spoke. While the others wore their pointy red elf hats vertically, the smug elf's hat tilted far to the side like those American servicemen's caps in World War Two photos. Out in the hall behind the elves there arose such a clatter, Kirby knew in a moment the elves must have brought eight reindeer.

"Sorry guys, no elves or reindeer this year. Check back after Thanksgiving next year."

The elf spokesman smiled elfishly, shook his fist and they winked out in a blink of Kirby's eyes.

Kirby closed his eyes again and waited. Nothing. Once more, he beseeched an idea to come to him. Nothing. He leaned back in his chair, eyes now wide open. Still nothing. Kirby slid the bottle of Jim Beam out of the bottom drawer, unscrewed the cap, and held out the bottle to the empty recliner as if toasting its invisible occupant. "If at first you don't succeed, try, try a different tack." He slugged down a large gulp and shook his head. Phew, strong stuff. Usually a bit more genteel, Kirby normally drank his Beam on the rocks in a crystal glass.

Three mice scurried out from the bookshelf. The smallest one, childlike, wore a tiny Santa hat. "No," Kirby said. "No mice this year either." The mice darted back into a baseboard corner escape route.

As he took another swig of Jim Beam the radio alarm in his bedroom switched on. But that couldn't be. He'd intended to set it for five p.m. Christmas Eve. He looked at his watch—five p.m. all right, but it was December twenty-third. "I must have set it on the wrong day," Kirby said aloud. He headed for the stairs to reset the alarm for the following day.

He'd planned to use the alarm because every year since the trapped coyote, Kirby had placed eight thick Kansas City strip steaks at the edge of the woods for *his* coyotes. Some years he watched them warily retrieve them. Some years they waited unseen until after dark. But he always left them on Christmas Eve. And he had begun to imagine that coyotes managed their own annual calendar, perhaps based on moon cycles. They seemed to know and anticipate the date.

Kirby walked through the open library doors and headed for the stairs. Behind him a voice called, "Or maybe *it is Christmas Eve.*"

Kirby stopped at the bottom step. He spun around and returned to the library.

"Christmastime is full of miracles," the voice said without inflection.

Kirby peered through the doorway. An old man in a nightshirt sat in Santa's chair. The man was translucent. Kirby could see the fabric of the recliner through the man's body.

"Ah, there you are. Come in, Brady Kirby. Pull up a chair."

Shit. Another waste of time. "And who are you supposed to be? Ebenezer Scrooge?"

"In life I was his partner, Jacob Marley," the apparition said, but he rattled no chains. He didn't even wear any. "You will be haunted by Three Spirits, Brady Kirby. The first at the stroke of midnight. The second at—"

"Whoa. Wait a second. I like *A Christmas Carol* as well as the next guy. I've seen at least ten versions of it in theatres and on TV." Kirby walked into the library and stood before the partially transparent interloper. "Your story is worn and tired, my friend. And I'm not going to try to write a fresh version. So be gone with you, Mr. Marley."

"Well, you don't have to be so rude." The apparition disapparated.

The radio still blared and Kirby trotted up the stairs. As he neared the top step, a deejay came on the air saying, *that was Burl Ives having a Holly Jolly Christmas. It's five-oh-seven p.m. on Christmas Eve, and kids, Santa's been spotted on radar over Canada. He's headed this way. So you be sure and get to bed early or*—Kirby reached the radio and shut off the chattering voice.

Very strange. Kirby knew it to be December twenty-third, yet the radio guy said it was a full day later. He pulled out his cell phone and activated it. On his home page, unmistakably posted in the upper right hand corner, was 12/24/2015, 5:09 p.m.

"How could I have completely spaced out a whole day?"

"Like I said, Christmastime is full of miracles, always has been since the very first one." The filmy visage of Jacob Marley lay spread out on Kirby's bed.

Marley's hands were crossed on the pillow underneath his head. Though Marley seemed comfortable, the quilt showed no indentation for his weight.

"You again." Kirby rolled his eyes dramatically for the benefit of his ghostly visitor.

"Yes, Brady Kirby, me again."

Kirby backed away from the bed toward the door. He folded his arms. "What do you want, Mr. Marley? And don't give me any of that three spirit shit. Okay?"

"Very well, no three ghost *shit*, as you say." Marley stretched fully, his fingers touching the headboard and his toes pointed at the end of the bed. "Nice bed."

"It's a Tempurpedic."

"Almost worth becoming flesh and blood again." Marley wiggled his body on the mattress. "Now, where was I? Oh yes, God has plans for you, Brady Kirby."

"I don't believe in God."

"Doesn't matter. He very much believes in you. And He *does* like your Christmas stories. They touch on what people should feel at Christmas, and how they should live their lives the year 'round."

"He said that?"

"Hardly. God does not need to *talk*. Yet He *does* make his will known. And that is why I am here."

"To make His will known?"

"Yes, that is rather the reason why I have come. Tell me why you set your alarm."

Kirby shook his head. "No. First you tell me how you skipped December twenty-third."

"Oh my heavens, I did not do that. But rest assured, it *was* done." The specter smiled a warm smile, bad teeth notwithstanding. "Now about the alarm?"

"You seem to know everything, don't you already know why?"

"Yes, but I want to hear you say it."

"Okay, if it will send you on your way sooner, I'll play your little game."

"It will,"

"All right. Every Christmas Eve since I saved the coyote's life I leave steaks for them out at the edge of the woods."

"*You* saved the coyote's life?"

Kirby's jaw clenched. "Yes."

Marley's smile widened. "Well you most certainly had a role in it. And why did *you*, at great personal risk, try to save the animal?"

Kirby glanced down at his sneakers, then moved his gaze around the bedroom. "Don't know. I guess I felt sorry for him."

"Ah, compassion." Marley nodded his head, his eyes glistened unnaturally, maybe even glowed as he looked upward. "And why do you still give the coyotes steak on Christmas Eve?"

"I don't know for sure why I do that either. I guess I feel like they are my coyotes in my woods...."

"And...?"

"Well, I guess you would say I love them."

"It does not matter what I would say. What do *you* say, Brady Kirby?"

"Yeah, okay, I love those coyotes. I do love them."

"Eureka, Mr. Kirby. *Love and compassion.* Two favorite words of the One whose birthday we celebrate." Marley rose off the bed without using his arms or legs, a nifty trick.

He floated to a standing position on the far side of the bed. "But you must remember, those words are not solely about animals. People thrive on love and compassion, too."

Marley slowly and dramatically raised his hand as if he played a ghost in a Scrooge movie, and pointed toward the window. "It looks as if it's almost dark, Brady Kirby. Is there something you must do?"

"Oh shit. Gotta feed my coyotes. I'll be right back."

Then Kirby hesitated. "You're real aren't you? You're not part of my storyteller's imagination. Right?"

161

"I am as real as you want me to be. Now, your coyotes are waiting and they, too, may have a story to tell."

"Be right back," Kirby bounded down the stairs, threw open the fridge, and pulled out the butcher-wrapped steaks. He flicked on the back yard light and stepped outside.

Kirby could see his breath and he hadn't even put on a jacket. But he didn't feel cold at all. He trod through the snow to the edge of the woods. There were no other tracks. He placed the KC strips in a row about fifteen feet apart along the edge of the woods.

After placing the last steak, he surveyed his work. Near the far end of the row two coyotes crept warily from the cover of the trees. There was enough light for Kirby to see the scarred, fur-free skin on the foreleg of the larger one—his coyote. They approached the nearest steaks. The smaller one—its mate, Kirby was sure—turned back toward the woods, tossing its head like a horse does shooing away flies.

Out scampered a tiny coyote pup no more than eight weeks old. It stumbled in the snow, tumbled and leaped back up. The moment the pup saw Kirby it stopped, then scurried under its mother's legs.

Kirby's coyote came toward Kirby, stopping about halfway. Kirby grinned at the way his coyote moved through snow, prancing so his feet plopped in and out without any drag. He looked like he was showing off. He showed no ill effects of his injury.

The coyote turned back to his mate. She nuzzled the pup, pushing him forward. The pup understood and raced to its father, and whereas the father had pranced like a hundred-thousand-dollar show horse, the pup navigated more like a snow plow.

As the pup neared its father, Kirby squatted down and softly clapped his hands. "Hey pup, com'ere. Come on, fella."

The pup looked back and forth between Kirby and its parents, and then slunk its way toward him, its tail hung low, dragging in the snow. Kirby kept chattering. The pup crept warily. Kirby toppled over on his side in the snow, and with Kirby' face now at pup's eye level, the pup pounced. They wrestled, and Kirby cuffed the pup, and the pup pawed Kirby and licked his face and chewed his fingers with tiny, needle sharp teeth.

The parents watched without moving. Three more coyotes appeared at the edge of the woods and stopped. The pup snowplowed its way back to his parents. Brady's coyote and his mate each picked up a single steak and disappeared into the trees, with the pup leaping and collapsing over and over, trying to dislodge the steak from its father's mouth.

Kirby realized the other animals would not approach their steaks while he was in the yard. He backed to the door and went inside. From the kitchen window he watched the others retrieve the meat. Some grabbed them and left, others wolfed them impossibly fast.

When the coyotes were gone Kirby remembered his guest upstairs and climbed the steps two at a time. He felt a draft as he neared his bedroom. Odd. Though the room felt cold, both the bedroom and master bath windows remained closed and locked. And there was no sign of Jacob Marley, nor any sign he had been there. Another of his literary apparitions no doubt.

In the library Kirby found nothing out of the ordinary, although the fire was nearly out. He stacked more logs on the embers and then sat down at his desk and clicked on his PC.

Kirby's Marley had said the coyotes might have a story to tell. He closed his eyes, scrunched them tight, and said, "What story?" His only answer came from the pop and crackle of green maple in the fireplace. He opened his eyes. Nothing. He sighed, flicked on his Bose radio to the Christmas music station.

Kirby tried to find the zone he got into when his writing flowed freely. Instead, he found himself enjoying the music. He even sang along. And he was still singing an hour later when Bing Crosby offered his rendition of "Little Drummer Boy." Kirby deepened his own voice to match Crosby's *rum pum pum pum.* When Crosby proudly sang *the ox and lamb kept time* the figurative bulb switched on, the library's fireplace blazed brighter.

Kirby began a new Word document.

And it came to pass in those days, that there went out a decree from Caesar Augustus, that all the world should be taxed. And Joseph also went up from Galilee, out of the city of Nazareth, into Judaea, unto the city of David, which is called Bethlehem; (because he was of the house and lineage of David). To be taxed with Mary his espoused wife, being great with child.

In the hills above Bethlehem the coyotes watched the man lead his donkey, the man's mate perched upon the donkey's back. The alpha male turned to his mate and his pup. "Her pup will soon be born. These are the humans about whom we have been foretold...

Two hours later Kirby finished his story. He reread it. It was pretty good. Somewhere good old Jacob Marley smiled, Kirby thought. And who knows, maybe even God.

The Limited

Alexis Grant felt like a grownup though she was only five. She and her mother walked side by side, each pulling identical travel bags, only Alexis's was half-sized. Their bags' plastic wheels clacked noisily as they crossed each seam in the gray marble entryway.

Chicago Union Station was the biggest building she'd ever entered, bigger than anything in Sioux City. It had been an adventurous day; her first bus ride (on a bus named after a dog), her first ever ride in a taxicab (the man spoke like he was from a foreign country), and now this.

***

On the taxi ride to Union Station, Alexis had asked the man why he talked funny. Her momma scolded her, and said she knew better and should be polite. Alexis guessed she should. But the man laughed.

"I am from Indian," is what she heard.

"Are you a Sioux Indian?" Alexis asked. Her momma smiled.

"No dear girl, I am not a Native American. I am from a country called India."

It was a good thing the man explained, because Alexis was very confused. Then her momma and the Indian talked about boring stuff so Alexis opened her *Curious George* book. At the station her momma paid the Indian man, and he helped them get their bags. At home, Momma had shown her how to slide the handle out of her bag, and she expertly did so. Her momma nodded and the man said, "Good job, little lady," in his funny voice, and then waved goodbye. He was nice.

Outside the cab, Alexis looked at the station. It was so big. And it looked like the buildings in her Children's Bible, with all of those round pillar things. They paused outside while her momma smoked a cigarette, and then they had hurried in, giggling as they went.

***

Danna Grant held the vestibule double doors open for her daughter. They stepped into the Great Hall. Danna watched her daughter absorb the scene. Lexie's eyes were wide, her mouth open. Danna recognized the wonder there, and she recalled her first time at the station. She had been seven or eight years old when she first stepped into the hall, older than her daughter now, but she'd still felt that sense of wonder. "What do you think, sweetie?"

"It's magic," her daughter said. "Like a wizard's palace. Oh, Momma, it's beautiful."

"There's over a thousand windows up there," Danna said of the enormous arched glass ceiling.

"How do they clean them, Momma?" Alexis said, gawking at the windows sixty feet above them.

"Very carefully."

They both laughed.

"We've got over an hour before we board the Capital Limited," Danna said. "We might as well have a seat on one of the pews."

"They're like at our church."

Danna nodded. "Yep, just like 'em."

***

Alexis parked her bag next to Momma's, pulled out her *Merry Christmas, Curious George* book, and climbed up on the pew. Her feet dangled, not reaching the marble floor. She swung her legs to and fro like she did on the jungle gym at the park. She looked around at all of the people walking in and out, and the ones sitting and waiting like they were.

There were men and women in uniforms, uniforms like the one her daddy wore in the photo at home. A family of four sat facing them on another pew not too far away. They dressed funny. The man wore a black, flat-brimmed hat and had a bushy beard. He was dressed in black except for a white shirt buttoned up until it disappeared beneath his beard. The woman wore a long, long dress and a bonnet like women wore in cowboy movies. The girl dressed just like the momma, and the boy just like his daddy except he only had a few whiskers on his chin.

Alexis pointed at them. "Look at those people, Momma!"

"Shh," her momma said. "It's not nice to point."

The woman and the girl across from them smiled.

Alexis tilted her head, nodding vigorously in their direction and whispered, "Why are they dressed that way?"

Her momma put her arm around her and pulled her close. "They're Mennonites, dear."

"What kind of knights?"

Momma chuckled. "Not knights who wear armor. Mennonite is a religion, like Catholics, or like we are Methodists. They dress that way because it helps them serve God."

"Do they believe in Christmas?" Alexis said, holding up her *Curious George Christmas* book.

"Yes, dear, they do, only in a slightly different way."

Alexis held out her book, front facing outward, and across the floor the girl with the bonnet smiled again.

"Don't bother them, Lexie."

"Okay." She opened her book to the first page.

***

Danna looked at her watch. Was the Capital Limited was running late? God, she needed a cigarette. "Come on, Lexie. Our train will board soon, I'll show you the platforms where all of the trains come in. Momma needs a smoke."

She took her daughter's hand, and they towed their bags behind them. The station was huge. It was a long walk. The platform seemed to bring more wonder for her daughter. Seven tracks, each separated by a raised platform, trailed out from the station. Three had trains in various stages of boarding and unloading. Her daughter was so excited she virtually tap-danced.

"Stay where I can see you, and don't go near the tracks," Danna told Alexis. Danna lit a Marlboro and watched her daughter cautiously explore. Alexis approached one of the tracks, paused and looked back at her. Danna nodded, signifying it was okay. Alexis took two small steps forward and again looked at her mother. Danna shook her head, and Alexis took one step back. Danna smiled and nodded again.

She watched her daughter toe an imaginary line, lean forward, and peer over the edge of the platform at the tracks below. Danna's cigarette reached its last roundup and she searched for an ashtray. Spying one by the automatic doors leading inside, she headed that way.

As she ground the butt out in the sand, a soothing female voice announced, "Pre-board passengers may begin boarding the Capital Limited on track three." They were in luck. Track three was less than a hundred feet away.

"C'mon, Lexie, that's us." Her daughter performed a brief river-dance on the platform and hurried to retrieve her bag.

On board the train in their sleeper compartment, Danna reflected how much smaller it was than she remembered. But Lexie seemed ecstatic, and peppered her with non-stop questions—what all of the buttons were for (lights, fan, call for assistance), can we open the windows (no), can we close this door (yes, it slides closed for privacy if we want), where do they put our beds (bunk beds, the top folds down from the wall, see? and our seats change into the bottom bed), how do we keep from falling out of the top bunk when the train bounces (there's a safety net), "Cool, a safety net, can I sleep up there," (yes), and on and on.

***

By the time their train departed, the conductor, Alberto Perez, had already visited their cabin and explained restrooms and showers, the dining car and lots of stuff. He kept talking and talking, and by the end Alexis only half-listened. But she did pay attention when Mr. Perez told them about the observation car. Alexis was not familiar with the word "observation" but Mr. Perez's detailed description of the car sparked her imagination.

As soon as the conductor moved on to the next compartment, Alexis said, "Can we go to the observation"—she carefully enunciated it—"car?"

"Not now, sweetie. After we get out of the city." Momma said.

"Can we go to the dining car?"

"No, Lexie. It's only three-thirty. Our dinner reservation isn't until six."

Alexis opened her *Curious George Christmas* book. She was bored, was sorry she only brought one book. Across from her, Momma opened a Tana French book. Momma said it was about people murdering people in Dublin. Dublin was in Ireland, Momma said, an island near England, which was where the Queen lived.

Alexis wasn't bored for long. The magic of the train, the way it swayed, the click of the tracks, the scenery of a big, urban city different from what they had seen on the bus, mesmerized her. Multi-colored graffiti on buildings, and... well, on everything, particularly enthralled her.

A voice came out of a speaker on the wall of their cabin. He spoke about a lot of things, many of them Mr. Perez had already told her momma. It was grownup stuff. She tuned out.

***

The engineer's announcements to the passengers raised a giant red flag for Danna. Smoking was strictly forbidden on the train, which Danna had anticipated.

The crux of her problem followed the "prohibited" announcement. Though the train would make numerous brief stops, there would be only four stops where passengers could get off and smoke. A twenty-hour trip—if the train remained on schedule which was unlikely—and only four smoke breaks. Not good. They weren't even out of Chicago and she craved one. The first break, South Bend, was two hours away. Not good at all. Danna touched the Marlboro package in her purse and bit her lower lip.

***

Alexis saw houses and lawns, and then farmland. "Can we go to the oddvacation car now?"

"Ob-sur-vay-shun," Momma corrected.

"Observation?"

Her momma closed her book with a pop. "Yep, let's do it."

The observation car was stacked on top of a regular one. It was covered in glass so you could even see the sky above. Alexis watched farms and houses scroll by below them. She felt like a bird flying above the train. "Oh, Momma. It's beautiful."

"Yes, it is. We're in Indiana now."

"A different state?"

"Yep."

"Have I ever been to Indiana?"

"Nope."

"Cool."

The man came on the loudspeaker saying, "Ladies and gentlemen, for those passengers who will be boarding and disembarking, we're about to make a very brief stop in La Porte, Indiana. This is *not* a smoking stop." Alexis glanced at her momma because Momma liked to smoke cigarettes. Momma kept her gaze on the rows of corn speeding by. But she *was* smiling.

The train slowed as it entered La Porte. Alexis waved to three boys in winter coats straddling bicycles at a crossing, watching the train pass. Two of them waved back and the third held up a finger, something Momma had said was not nice to do. They passed a high school with a football field, but there was nobody around because Christmas was only two days away.

The family who dressed funny came into the car and sat on the other side. The boy and girl were talking.

Her momma nudged her. "Stop staring," she whispered.

Alexis turned back to the windows on her side. The train had passed through the town.

***

Danna leaned over and told her daughter to wait in her seat in the observation car, while she went to the restroom. First, she grabbed her pack of Marlboros from their cabin. She met Alberto Perez in the passageway by their cabin.

"Mr. Perez, we're coming up on South Bend and I plan to get off and have a smoke. Is there someone in the observation car who can keep an eye on my daughter, Lexie?"

"Si, ma'am, Mr. Potter is the steward up there. Mr. Potter will be happy to assist you. He'll be wearing a coat like mine."

Danna thanked him, made her stop at the train's miniscule restroom. Like airlines, decals that forbade smoking were plastered throughout the tiny space. No problem. She could wait. Upon exiting she set off in search of Mr. Potter.

***

Alexis watched cars on a road that ran alongside the train. One, a red one that looked very fast seemed to pace her. She pretended they were in a race. The red car began to pull ahead. Then Momma appeared with a man. The man was shorter than her momma, and wore

171

a train man's uniform. His little round glasses pushed down on his nose.

Alexis stood and entered the aisle, giving her mother a big hug. "We were racing a red car but it was too fast," she said pointing outside.

"Lexie, this is Mr. Potter. He's the steward of the observation car and the café below. South Bend is coming up soon, and I'm going to have a smoke," her momma said. "Mr. Potter will keep an eye on you while I'm on the platform. You be sure and stay right here."

"Okay, Momma. Pleased to meet you, Mr. Potter."

"The pleasure's all mine, Miss Lexie."

"Do you need to go potty before we stop?" her momma asked.

Alexis blushed. "No, Momma."

***

Danna thanked Mr. Potter and sat next to her daughter on the couch-like bench facing outward. The Capital Limited had entered the suburbs of South Bend. She craved a smoke, and for the millionth time vowed to quit, this time as soon as she got through the holidays.

The engineer's voice came over the loudspeakers. "Ladies and gentlemen, we are approaching the South Bend station where we will stop for fifteen minutes. If you wish to smoke, now is the time to do so. Please exit the train, but remain on the platform. The conductor will notify you when we are about to depart. Thank you."

As The Limited slowed for its approach to the station, Danna stood, anxious to light up. "Okay, Lexie, you be good. I'll be back in a few minutes."

"Okay, Momma," Lexie said without shifting her gaze from the old brick buildings of downtown South Bend.

By the time the train came to a full stop Danna was at the door waiting. If she hurried, she might get two cigarettes in.

On the platform, she tapped one out. The package felt nearly empty. Once she had that first big inhale, she checked her pack—only one left. Damn. Okay, change of plans. She would quickly smoke the one, and then go into the station and grab another pack.

"Sorry, ma'am, we don't sell cigarettes here," the man at Amtrak counter said. "There's a grocer across the street that does."

Danna thanked the man and hustled across the street. She purchased two packs and as she exited the store she heard two shrill blasts. Her train! A parked bus loading passengers blocked her path and delayed her sprint across the street. When she had a clear view of the station, she saw her train begin to move. No!

"Wait! Wait!" But by the time she reached the platform the last half dozen cars rolled by, picking up speed. Three cars from the end, her daughter, mouth open, watched Danna stand helplessly on the platform. Lexie's right hand pressed against window glass in the semblance of a wave.

***

Alexis spent the time parked at the station watching the other people in the observation car. Mother and daughter—the funny-dressed ones—were sewing. The man and son were reading books. It looked like the man had a Bible. He held it close, like he couldn't see very well. As she watched, the boy looked up from his book and caught her staring. He touched the brim of his hat. Embarrassed, Alexis turned away.

There was an old couple, older even than Pop and Grammy, who lived in Washington DC. Pop and Grammy were Alexis's daddy's parents. Her daddy died in Afa-gana-stana when she was only two. Alexis pretended that she remembered him, but she didn't really. All she had were the photos, and the stories Momma and Pop and Grammy told her.

There was a man in the corner who had on a uniform like her daddy wore in the photo at home. It looked like he was asleep. Two boys sat across from him, their heads down punching buttons on their phones. Alexis wished she had one, but Momma said she was way too young. Momma said that a lot.

A train whistle blew twice and the conductor guy motioned people to get back on. Momma must already be on, maybe down in their little room. Now the train began to move, slowly at first, but picking up steam, which Momma said means going faster. And there was Momma now, on the platform shouting and waving her hands. But the train didn't stop. Alexis pressed her nose and hand against the glass. "Momma," she whispered.

***

Danna wasted little time watching the train pull away. She marched into the station and up to the ticket counter. A young man hunched over the counter reading *The Observer*, the Notre Dame Student newspaper. He must not have seen her approach. She cleared her throat.

Startled, he haphazardly folded the newspaper. "Sorry," he said. "May I help you?"

"Yes, I got off the Capital Limited to get a pack of cigarettes and it left without me."

The young man—the placard on his shirt pocket identified him as Brett—shook his head. "Gee, sorry, that happens from time to time. Let me see..." he ran his finger up and down a printout. "You headed to D.C.?"

"Yes, I am."

"Yeah, okay. The Capital Limited will be back through here on its way to D.C. at around five-fifteen tomorrow afternoon, Christmas Eve. I can get you ticketed for that one, and you will be there by lunchtime on Christmas Day."

Danna sucked in a deep breath and exhaled. "My five-year-old daughter is alone on *that* train," she said, pointing east down the tracks.

"Oh shit." The young man's face turned crimson either from the word that slipped out, or the predicament he found himself as ticket agent.

Danna watched his eyes dart back and forth as he thought.

"Look, ma'am. There's no way they can turn the train around." Brett held up a finger. "The stationmaster is off for the holidays, but we'll figure something out, and I can call Chicago who can communicate what's happened to The Limited. I can assure you that The Limited's staff will take good care of..."

"Lexie... Alexis Grant, berth four twenty-one."

"They'll take good care of Alexis. Let me make a call to the airport," he said. "We don't have a lot of commercial flights, but they've increased for the holidays. Maybe we can get you caught up to The Limited on down the line."

"Thank you, Brett. I'm Danna, Danna Grant."

"Okay, Danna, why don't you have a seat while I make some phone calls?"

***

Alexis watched her run into the station as train trailed away. What now? What would Momma want her to do? Find Mr. Potter. No. Stay put and wait until Mr. Potter comes by again.

The sun began to set beyond the windows on her side of the car. Pink and orange streaks across a purple background. Pretty. She watched the colors change ever so slightly. Alexis realized she was very hungry. She and Momma were supposed to go to the dining car at six. Alexis didn't have a watch, but she *was* learning how to tell time.

"Beautiful sunset, huh?"

Startled, Alexis turned toward the voice.

The army man was awake and had taken a seat near hers. He was a stranger. Alexis didn't speak to strangers. She pretended he wasn't even there.

"Ah, your mother told you not to talk to strangers. Good for her."

Alexis watched the sky begin to grow darker.

"This kind of sunset reminds me of Disney movies."

Alexis wanted to ask which Disney movies, for she had seen a lot of them. She didn't though.

"I have a daughter just about your age. She's five. I haven't seen her for a long time."

"I'm five, too," Alexis said, and then clamped her hand over her mouth. She turned away from the army man and watched the colorful sky.

"That's okay. I won't tell your mother you spoke to me. Our secret."

Out of the corner of her eye Alexis saw the man look at his watch. She swiveled his way ever so slightly.

"Well it's time for my reservation in the dining car," the man said. "It was nice talking to you, young lady."

She watched him stand. He winked, and headed for the car's exit.

"There you are." It was Mr. Potter. He squeezed by the army man in the narrow aisle. Mr. Potter sat next her.

"We've heard from your mother, Alexis. She got left behind in South Bend. They're working to help her catch up with us in Toledo."

Alexis didn't know where that was. She nodded her head solemnly.

"Now, in the meantime, Mr. Perez and I are going to take good care of you. And that starts with dinner. Come with me to the dining car." He held out his hand and she placed her tiny hand in his great big one.

Almost all of the booths were filled. One near the rear had only three people, an older couple and her army man. Mr. Potter guided her to that table.

"Hello, everyone, do you mind if this young lady sits with you?" All of the grownups smiled. "This is Alexis."

George and Ellen were the older couple across from her, and her Army man's name was Peter St. John.

"Now Alexis, you stay put until I return for you, okay?" Mr. Potter had a nice smile. She liked him.

"Yes, sir, I will."

"Now we're not strangers anymore," said the Army man. He held out his hand, "How do you do, Miss Alexis?"

She took his hand and shook it like her momma taught her.

He pulled his hand away. "Ow, ouch, such strong grip!" He shook the hand as if to shake the pain away.

Everyone laughed, even her. She missed her momma, and down deep there lurked the fear of being without her, but at that moment she was having fun.

***

Brett, the college kid standing in for the South Bend stationmaster, was a godsend. He had contacted the train, Lexie was in good hands there. There were no applicable flights out of the local airport, but Brett had arranged with Enterprise to bring her a rental Buick LaCrosse.

She and her Buick cruised at seventy-nine in a seventy miles-per-hour speed limit on I-80 between Elkhart and Waterloo, Indiana. With any luck, she should make Toledo's union station ahead of The Limited.

As the mile markers clicked by she thought of David, and how much of him she saw in little Lexie. God, she missed him. Christmas with his folks this year would certainly bring at least one session of tears with her and June, David's mother. June and Tony Grant hadn't seen Lexie in over a year. She had grown so much. She was so bright and inquisitive, just like

David. And she had David's green eyes, and his lopsided grin.

The Grants will certainly see their David as a boy, in Lexie, too. Danna hadn't met David until their sophomore year at Iowa State. So, she never knew him as a kid. But she'd enjoyed flipping through the Grant's photo albums with David and his folks. They pointed to photos and told stories about them. Everyone laughed—like the time little Davy and his Cocker Spaniel puppy, Babe, played tug-o-war with one of Tony's slippers. The photo showed a kneeling Davy, his arm around a seated Babe, proudly holding up the slipper remains. David had pointed to the photo and said, "That picture was taken post-lecture."

It had been nearly three years since she held David, and kissed him goodbye as he left for his second tour of duty in Afghanistan. Maybe she would find another man to love someday. But she feared that every man, held up to her David, would be found wanting.

Danna shook off those thoughts, then turned up the volume on the radio's Christmas Music. Karen Carpenter crooned "Merry Christmas, Baby." No use. Holiday music only made her think of him. Would the pain ever end? Danna left the music volume loud, smiled (for she did love the music), and wiped tears with a Kleenex as the Buick passed slower cars, speeding on to Toledo.

***

Their dinners had arrived. George and Ellen each had the steak. George ordered his medium-rare, whatever that meant, and Ellen told the waiter to burn hers black, which brought some laughter. Peter—he said to call him Pete—had salmon, which is a fish. Alexis had a corn dog and French fries.

The grownups asked her what grade she was in. She told them kindergarten. They asked lots of questions.

"Are you traveling alone?" Ellen asked.

"No. I'm with my momma. But she got off the train back there for a minute and the train left without her. I watched her running after us, but the train *picked up steam* and was too fast for my momma to catch." Alexis was pleased she got to use "picked up steam" in a sentence. Momma told her if you say a new word or phrase in a sentence three times it will be yours forever.

"Mr. Potter is taking care of me until my momma can get back on the train."

Mr. St. John smiled. "And how will she do that?"

"I don't know, but she's very smart." They all laughed, but Alexis didn't know why.

The old people asked Mr. St. John about his military service and he said he spent two tours in Afghanistan and was now stationed in Fort Riley, but she didn't listen where. He said he was with the Army first division—the Big Red One.

"My daddy was a red one soldier, too" Alexis said.

"Is he out of the service now?" George asked.

"Yes. He died."

Everyone stopped talking for a while. And then they asked more questions about where and when he died, and how much she must miss him. She answered them in just a few words because she didn't want to talk about it.

When Ellen said, "You must really miss him a lot," Alexis finished chewing her last bite of corn dog. Momma told her not to talk with her mouth full.

"My daddy died when I was two. I don't even remember him. But I do wish he was still here. Momma misses him a lot. And it would be nice to have a daddy."

Everybody got quiet again.

***

Danna pulled into a rest area just west of Toledo. She googled Toledo Union Station and entered its address into the Buick's GPS. She took a quick potty break to eliminate the two large coffees she'd consumed in South Bend and on the drive.

Back on I-80 the traffic was heavy, which she supposed was natural for December twenty-third. As she entered suburban Toledo, traffic turned from heavy to congested. She wanted to scream or lay on her horn. Instead she gripped the steering wheel in a white-knuckled death grip and chewed her lip. 8:05 her watch chastened.

***

They finished their desserts—Alexis had a brownie with a scoop of vanilla ice cream—and George, Ellen, and Mr. St. John got up to leave. Alexis scooted out to let Mr. St. John go, then she sat back down.

"Maybe we'll see each other again in the observation car," Mr. St. John winked at her as he left.

"Maybe." Alexis finished her milk. Then she got busy running her spoon back and forth on her dessert dish, each time gathering tiny amounts of crumb and melted vanilla.

"Who are you with, little girl?" Her waiter asked.

"I'm not a little girl. I'm Alexis and I'm five."

The waiter chuckled. "You here with your mother and father?"

Alexis didn't feel like telling the whole story again. "I'm waiting for Mr. Potter. He's going to come get me."

"Okay, young lady, we're going to need this table for the next group of reservations. Let me see if I can find Mr. Potter."

Alexis returned to her stray brownie crumb roundup.

***

Danna could see flashing lights of emergency vehicles ahead. Three lanes were narrowing down to two. Discourteous yay-hoos were speeding along the shoulder to pick up a few car lengths before they

180

merged. Traffic ahead tailgated to prevent the maneuver. *Tis the season.* Danna smiled at the thought. But when she got to the area where rude drivers tried to merge, she tailgated, too.

A white Escalade selected the slot in front of her to merge. She tried to prevent it. A part of her knew she could never stop if the car in front hit its brakes hard. The Escalade inched closer to the infinitesimally small gap. She closed it even more. Danna's fingers felt the pain of trying to squeeze her steering wheel out of existence. A critical moment arrived. It became clear that her adversary was willing to hit her car to win the contest. She tapped her brakes three quick times to warn the car behind she was slowing, and let the Escalade cut in. Then she flipped him the bird. Without turning around, the man gave her a thumbs up. The bastard.

***

Mr. Potter arrived shortly after Alexis spoke with the waiter. He took her back to the observation car.

"All right, Miss Grant. It's almost eight o'clock, and we're pulling in to Toledo. You stay here and enjoy the scenery. And either Mr. Perez or I will come get you in about an hour. We'll help you get your bed ready."

"Can I sleep in the top bunk?"

Mr. Potter grinned. "Why you'll have to ask Mr. Perez that."

***

Danna pulled into the station's pickup and drop off zone, but her gut—which could use a handful of Tums—told her she was too late. She shut off the Buick and started for the front doors.

"Ma'am. Ma'am! You can't park there," a man in a security uniform said, walking toward her.

Danna clenched her teeth. "Look, I just need to see if the Capital Limited has arrived. Then I'll be right back."

"Can't do it, Ma'am. Nobody can park here."

"What about all these others?" A giant internal cranial grandfather clock clanged out the seconds in her head.

"They're loading and unloading." The man wasn't angry or exasperated like she was. But he was firm.

"Okay, look, here's my keys." She pulled them and a twenty-dollar bill out of her purse. "My five-year-old daughter is on that train, alone and afraid." She placed the keys and the bill in his hand. "If you need to move it or tow it, be my guest."

She left him looking at the objects in his hand and shaking his head.

***

The train picked up steam out of the station. Alexis wondered if using the phrase in a thought counted the same as saying it. A town on the far edge of Toledo made a show of Christmas lights on their downtown buildings. It was pretty. She pressed her hands and face to the glass of the observation car.

"Beautiful, isn't it?"

She rotated her head keeping her forehead plastered to the glass. It was Mr. St. John. He was back in his seat near hers.

"Yes, it is. They are even prettier than the ones in my town."

"Which is?"

"Sioux City."

"Sioux City?" Mr. St. John cocked his head in a funny way.

"Yes. It's in Iowa."

Mr. St. John leaned back in his seat and looked up at the glass ceiling. There were no stars to see. Alexis turned back to the bright lights. The town had a square with a huge Christmas tree and a shining star.

***

Danna hurried out of the station. She had missed The Limited by twenty minutes. A quick glance showed her Buick still where she left it. The security guy was helping an older couple get their luggage out of a trunk. They thanked him and he turned.

"Hey! There you are. You did make it quick." He looked around. "No daughter?"

"The train had already pulled out. Do you know where it makes its next stop for any length of time?"

He nodded. "Yeah, Cleveland. It's an easy two-hour drive, but it'll take the train three. You better get going." He placed the keys in her palm.

She looked at the keys. The twenty was there with them. "Oh, no this is for you, for your help." Danna held out the twenty.

"You hang on to it for gas money," he said. "Now go catch up with your daughter. Oh, yeah, you two have a Merry Christmas."

***

"Alexis?"

She turned away from the tree. Mr. St. John wore a big grin.

"When we were introduced at dinner, the conductor only mentioned your first name." Mr. St. John clasped his hands and leaned forward on his elbows. "Is your last name Grant?"

"Yes."

"And your dad's name was Dave?"

"No. It was David," Alexis said. She wondered how Mr. St. John knew so much. She was beginning to feel a little bit scared.

"And your dad called you Lexie."

"I ... I don't remember."

"Oh, he did. You see, Lexie, your dad and I not only served in the same unit in Afghanistan, we were bunkmates. And he was my best friend."

He held out his hands, beckoning for hers. Alexis was wary, but her hands were not, and he took them, softly squeezing.

"I've known you since you were a baby. You were born in May, a month after my Wendy. Your dad and I exchanged the photos we got from home and from the internet." He paused and swallowed hard.

He released her hands and raised his in the air like a movie cowboy held a gun on him. "And you and I have met before tonight. A few weeks... a few weeks before your dad was killed. I met you and your mom on Skype. I remember how beautiful your mom was and how pretty you were—still are. You spoke mostly gibberish." Mr. St. John smiled. "But you kept pointing to the screen and saying daddy just as plain as day."

Alexis lower lip quivered. She didn't want to cry but worried she would. Maybe Mr. St. John noticed, for he leaned back in his seat and watched the winter night's landscape roll by outside.

"Mr. St. John?"

"Oh, no. Your dad would put me in his famous armlock if he knew I let you call me Mr. St. John. You call me Pete."

***

Danna camped in Interstate 80's passing lane. Though the speed limit was seventy, Danna pushed ninety when traffic allowed. She never drove this fast, and she realized one little mistake and she, and perhaps some innocent, were toast. But she had to beat that damned train.

She braked hard when some lout crept along in the passing lane, pacing the cars to his right. She tailgated and he got the message, sped up around the slow cars and then pulled in the right lane with them. Danna tromped the Buick accelerator and it lurched forward, eighty-five, and back to ninety. But then something changed.

Was it the air temperature in the Buick? Or her imagination? The hairs on her neck prickled. And she imagined David sitting next to her. It was not him, or his Christmas ghost, but he was there *inside* her, *beside* her. David sat next to her, watching her, wearing that cockeyed boyish grin. "*She needs her mother alive, Dan.*" Danna nodded and David disappeared. She backed off the pedal and set the cruise control for seventy-nine.

***

"Pete?"

"Yes, Lexie?"

"Was he a nice man?"

"The best. A good man. Everyone in the platoon liked him. He was the best friend I ever had. Or ever will have. And your dad was the bravest man I ever met."

"My momma showed me his bravery medals."

"Did she tell you how he earned them?"

Alexis shook her head. "No. Only that he was a hero." Alexis wasn't used to talking about her daddy without her momma. Where was she? Alexis's adventure alone on the train had begun to change. Had it become a nightmare? She sometimes had bad dreams. But Momma was always there for her. She leaned back in her seat and dropped her gaze to her knees. She felt tears coming.

"Lexie, your father saved my life."

She turned to look at Mr. St. John. It looked like he might have tears coming, too.

"My life, and Bill Ott's."

She was all ears—something her momma often said.

"Your father, Tommy Smithers, Bill and I were returning to base when a rocket hit our Humvee.

Tommy was killed, and Bill and I badly hurt—see the scar on my chin and neck?"

She did see it, in fact she had been trying not to look at it for quite a while. The scar started at the tip of his chin and ran around the side of his neck. "Yes, I do. Can I touch it, Mr. St. John?"

"Pete. Call me Pete. And yes, go ahead." He leaned forward, sticking his chin out. He was smiling now, no longer near tears."

She traced her finger along the scar, and cringed.

"It doesn't hurt anymore. But it did then, and the ones who shot the rocket were coming up the road in, and behind a big truck. Bill and I couldn't even hold a rifle. But your dad was cool. He called for air-evacuation, and began firing back."

Alexis watched Pete's expression, and listened with growing pride.

"Your dad could have, should have, ducked out the back and disappeared into the scrub brush and trees on the roadside behind us." His eyes filled again as he paused. "But not Dave. He wasn't leaving us. By the time the Cobra helicopters arrived he had been hit three times but was still firing."

Now Alexis began to cry. She was sad. But she was happy, too. Happy that her daddy was so brave. And she was proud.

"Your dad died that night at the base hospital. But Bill and I are alive because of him.

Pete slid over and put his arm around her. "It's okay, Lexie. Let it out." He squeezed her shoulder. She looked up at him. His lower lip and the scar on his chin quivered. "I get to spend Christmas with my little girl, Wendy, thanks to Dave."

They watched dark trees and fields whiz by outside.

"But even though you cannot see him, your dad is with you always. And he is so proud of you."

***

Danna was making good time when it began to snow, lightly at first. Then the wind picked up, and with it, the size of the snowflakes.

"Really? Snow? Are you kidding me?!"

"Chill, Dan. You're the best winter driver in Sioux City. You can handle this."

Danna knew David wasn't really there, that her imagination had placed him next to her. And what he said was only what she thought would likely come from him were he there. But he was a comfort, nonetheless. She longed for his flesh and blood knee resting beside hers so she could clasp it and feel him place his hand on hers. The loss still tore at her sometimes.

"Damn you, David. Why'd you die?"

No answer.

She had to catch up with Lexie in Cleveland. The worry ate at her. She should have picked up Tums at the station in Toledo.

If she didn't catch the train, at some point she would have to contact June and Tony to meet Lexie's train in D.C. And what would David's parents think of her then?

"They will think you're the same lovable, scatterbrained girl I married. They already know what a wonderful mother you are." Danna swiveled quickly. No one there. But she swore it was not her channeling an imaginary David. It was his voice, his inflection, his chuckle.

She turned back to the road. At this point the snow wasn't sticking on the Interstate, just passing across. Maybe she would luck out.

***

"So, Lexie, what do you want for Christmas?"

They had been sitting quietly for a while watching car lights on a nearby highway. Pete said it was most likely the eye-eighty highway.

"I want a puppy, but Momma says I'm too young."

187

"I see."

"But it's not fair."

"Why is that?"

I've seen pictures in a book at Grammy June's and Grandy Tony's.

"Dave's folks in Arlington?"

"Yes. And when Daddy was little like me *he had* a puppy dog. It was a cockerel spaniard."

"Named Babe."

Alexis jaw dropped. "How'd you know?"

"Soldiers have a lot of time to talk. Even more so when they are bunkmates. And best friends. We talked about more than you and Wendy, you know." He mussed her hair.

She didn't mind. It felt good. Did her daddy ever muss her hair?

"He talked a lot about growing up with Babe. And I had a Labrador as a kid. Her name was Runner.

"What a funny name?"

"It described her to a 'T.'"

"Oh, look, Pete! It's snowing."

***

The snow began to stick on the pavement. The wind created little snow stripes. Soon those stripes would become ridges. Ridges became problematic. As they grew they would evolve from annoyances to hazards.

"Chill, babe, you've handled worse on the drive to and from Des Moines."

Danna laughed out loud. She remembered when he first called her "babe," and she had accused him of not loving her, but only wanting to replace his boyhood pet. It became a running joke in their relationship, both extending clever parries and thrusts. David had even taken to giving her commands. "Sit," he'd say. "Stay." God, how she had loved him … how she missed him so much, even now.

After going around a pickup the Buick briefly lost traction, wobbling as she returned to the outside lane.

"You're making great time, babe. Back off on the speed just a bit."

She didn't look to see if he was there beside her. "How do you know we won't run into a big traffic jam?"

"How do you know we will?"

She smiled, and almost continued the banter. The dashboard clock confirmed she was making good time. Danna dropped the cruise control from seventy-nine to seventy-two.

Her shoulders and arms ached, a common factor of winter driving. A person tenses, knowingly or not, the body stays ready for quick action, for any eventuality. If only David would rub her shoulders. But he could not. This David was ephemeral, a figment, or as Ebenezer Scrooge once bluntly stated, "a bit of undigested potato." Danna removed her right hand from the wheel and rubbed her left shoulder. After a time, she swapped hands and rubbed the other one. A solo massage.

By the mile markers she was only forty minutes from the west edge of Cleveland. Good news. She pulled out her cell phone and dialed the number Amtrak had given her.

"Really, Dan? You're going to drive one-handed in a snow storm and make a call with the other?"

Danna gave her imaginary husband a smarmy smile.

***

"Hello, senorita Grant."

It was Mr. Perez. Alexis and Pete had been talking about kindergarten, and how hers differed from Wendy's. They were laughing and Pete teased her, and almost made her forget her momma was not there.

"Hello," Alexis said.

"The train has been in contact with your mother. She plans to catch up with us soon." Mr. Perez put his hands on his knees and leaned toward her. "But your mother says it's past your bedtime."

Alexis looked at Pete, then turned to Mr. Perez. "May I please sleep in the top bed?"

Mr. Perez stood up straight and placed his hands on his hips. "Ah, and so polite."

"She sure is, and smart as a whip," Pete said.

Alexis didn't know about smart whips, but she could tell Pete was being nice.

"I think we can accommodate your request, mija. Come with me and we'll see to your berth."

Gosh, sometimes she couldn't understand everything grownups said. But if she pretended to understand, things usually worked out. So, she hugged Pete and told him she would see him in the morning and went with Mr. Perez to see what her 'birth' would be like.

As they reached the car's pneumatic door, Mr. Perez stopped and turned. "Shall I prepare your berth, Mr. St. John?"

"No, I think I'll enjoy the night view for a while."

Alexis watched Mr. Perez unfold a bed out of the wall well above her head. He attached things here and there, then turned to her.

"Do you have jammies?"

"Yes, in there." She pointed to her bag under the seat.

"All right. I'm going to step outside and slide this door closed. And you latch it like this, see? And slide this curtain closed. Okay?"

She nodded solemnly.

"Then you get into your jammies and open the door. I'll be right outside."

She nodded again and he stepped out. Alexis decided on her Spiderman jammies. Then Mr. Perez had Alexis retrieve her toothbrush and toothpaste, and escorted her to the tiny restroom. He was waiting.

"Okay, mija, let's get you to bed."

"What's a mija?"

"It's a Spanish word for someone you like very much."

"Are you going to wrap me up in that net to keep me from falling?"

Mr. Perez laughed loudly. "You'll see, mija."

***

As I-80 entered the outskirts of Cleveland the volume of traffic increased some. Traffic kept the outside lane relatively snow free, but the passing lane was covered in hard-packed snow. Traction in that lane was minimal. Danna had neither seen nor heard a peep from her ephemeral husband since they reached the city's first suburb.

The Buick's clock compared to the distance yet to the terminal gave Danna a bit of a cushion, so she moved with the flow of traffic. She only passed the slowest vehicles that everyone was passing. With slower speeds, she found it necessary to use the Buick's wipers on the plump 'Hallmark Channel'-style snowflakes. In Elyria she took the ramp onto I-480 into the heart of downtown. Traffic continued to slow. Snow piled. Danna worried.

***

Alexis lay in bed on her side looking at the net. It was like the net Julie down the street had to keep them from falling off Julie's trampoline. Alexis was crying. Crying about her daddy. Crying because her momma was not there. What if something happened to Momma like what happened to Daddy? What if the last time she ever saw Momma was when she ran along the platform after Alexis' train? What if some day she didn't remember Momma either? And she only knew her from stories people told her, like Pete told about her daddy.

***

Danna had turned onto northbound US 77 a few minutes earlier. The outside lane had been plowed and treated, but the inside lane was perilous. Only a few lunatics chose to defy death. Danna crept along the outside lane with all of the sane drivers. Her anxiety gradually turned to anger. "Not again," she murmured. She could use some her husband's calm clarity.

Danna crossed the Cuyahoga River and the highway rose into the heights on the river's north side. She could see Lake Erie! The tracks ran along its shores— two, maybe three miles.

Meanwhile the cars rolled along like some never-ending funeral procession. She considered taking the next exit and scooting along the back streets. Danna smiled. If David were here he would say, "Think about it, babe. If the snow is bad on the highway, how would it be on the back streets? Those streets most likely won't see a plow for days, those streets you know nothing about in a city you've never been in until a half hour ago."

"Okay. Okay." Danna said out loud to the rental car interior.

***

Alexis' tears dwindled away as the fatigue of a long day, the longest day she could ever remember, made her eyes heavy. She dreamt of Santa Claus, and of her father.

***

Danna turned left from Superior Avenue onto East Ninth which dropped steeply to the waterfront and the tracks. She could see the terminal's Grand Tower tantalizingly near. At an intersection, literally five blocks from her destination, a Toyota had tried to turn uphill from St. Clair Avenue and lost traction in the middle of the intersection. Danna tapped the Buick's brakes nonstop as it nosed toward the half dozen cars affected. She stopped in time. But stopped she was. Danna wished she knew some kind of yoga mind calming exercises. While she waited, several teenage boys from one of the affected cars braved the weather and began to push the original offender. Thank God for teenage boys. Once they got the Toyota headed up the hill, they moved to the next car, and then the next.

Finally, she could continue down Ninth. As she passed the boys loading into an old Crown Victoria, she tapped her horn and blew them a kiss. One waved back as he held the door for his pals.

The station's lot was only half full. She found a spot fairly near the entrance. As she put the Buick in park, she felt a hand—David's hand—squeeze her leg.

"You made it, babe. You're a good girl. Yes, you are."

The pressure on her thigh evaporated as did the feeling of his presence. Danna squeezed her eyes tight, willing back the tears. She opened her eyes to the dark interior and the snow blowing across the parking lot light's glow outside.

After clicking the lock, she performed a slipping, sliding, sprint to the station's covered entrance. Out of habit she stomped the snow from her wet shoes and socks and hurried inside. She spotted the Amtrak desk across great hall.

Arriving at the desk, she was almost afraid to speak. "Has the Capital Limited already been through?"

The woman shook her head. "I'm sorry, ma'am."

No!

"The Limited has been delayed. It won't arrive for another half hour or so."

"Thank God." Danna exhaled, reached into her purse, fumbled around inside, and pulled out her ticket with a shaky hand. "Can you tell me if this ticket is still good? Or do I need to purchase another one to board."

The clerk examined it for a moment. Her expression changed and she brought her gaze up until her comically wide-open eyes met Danna's. "You're Mrs. Grant!"

Danna nodded.

The clerk, whose name tag identified her as Chris, grabbed Danna's shaky hand. "That's wonderful. Oh, that's wonderful. We hoped you would make it. I've gotta' call Amtrak!"

Danna held up the ticket. "What about this? Will this get me back on?"

The clerk laughed. "Oh, Mrs. Grant, there won't be any trouble getting you back on board."

Danna heard one side of the phone conversation. Chris, the clerk, was obviously thrilled to make the call. She giggled like a schoolgirl as she spoke to whomever. Danna felt like giggling, too. She had made it.

Chris told her The Limited was only ten minutes away. Mr. Perez would meet her at the steps to car nine.

"And I've spoken to Brett in South Bend. He helped you with the car rental," Chris said. "Amtrak will take care of returning your vehicle to Enterprise. All you need do is look for Mr. Perez and step on board."

***

Danna stood in the cold leaning against the station wall. She couldn't bear to wait inside. Though the platform's roof stood above her, the wind blew swirling snow around her feet, tiny snow tornados. She could hear The Limited's horn blasting at automobile crossings before she could see the train or its lights.

As the train rolled to a stop, Danna wondered which was car nine. She needn't have worried because Mr. Perez was the first to step off, before any other car doors opened. He held his jacket closed at the collar and tilted his head into the wind. Danna walked, almost ran toward him.

He spotted her and smiled. Danna returned his grin twofold. When she reached him, Danna wrapped him in a bear hug. "Am I glad to see you."

Mr. Perez looked sheepish. "Come, let's get in out of the wind. You don't have any bags do you?"

Danna shook her head and followed him inside. Her berth was upstairs, but he stopped at the foot of the narrow steps. "She's asleep in your berth, in the upper bunk."

Danna smiled at that. The little rascal got her upper bunk.

"I thought you might want to let her sleep... or surprise her and wake her yourself."

Danna hugged him even tighter, and kissed his cheek. Mr. Perez's sheepish look graduated to full blown embarrassment.

Outside Danna's berth Mr. Perez whispered, "You're still scheduled for breakfast at seven-thirty. Is that okay, or do you want me to move your reservation to a later time? I know you've had a long day."

***

In her dream, Alexis was all nestled asleep in her bed, waiting for Santa Claus. Though asleep, she had visions of Santa as he crept up to her bed. He bent over and kissed her cheek. Santa's hands were ice cold when he touched the sides of her cheeks. And he smelled of cigarettes and Momma's perfume. Alexis opened her eyes. "Momma!"

***

Lexie was back in the upper bunk, sound asleep. Danna had brought Lexie down to the lower bunk and held her tight. They each talked of their adventures. Danna was shocked that Pete St. John was aboard. She had not seen him since Pete had been released from Walter Reed Hospital. Lexie was a toddler then, and the pain of David's death was still hot and fresh for Danna.

195

Pete had tried to cheer her up with accounts of David's heroism, but Danna was inconsolable, and she suspected, rude. Eventually, Danna felt her adrenaline high wane. Her eyes grew heavy.

***

Danna and Alexis sat at the breakfast table. Apparently, they were somewhat celebrities to The Limited's wait staff. As they waited for their meals, Danna, bacon and eggs, and her daughter selected strawberry pancakes. Danna's stomach growled loudly. "I'm so hungry I could eat a horse." She said.

Alexis laughed. "Me too! And the saddle."

It was Danna's turn to laugh. Her little girl was not only bright, but witty. The humor and wit come from her father, Danna thought. Though she couldn't feel David or see him, she had the memory of last night.

As they finished breakfast Mr. Perez came through the dining car. "Mr. Perez?"

He stopped at their table. He rubbed Alexis hair. "Did you enjoy the hotcakes, mija?"

"Yes, Mr. Perez. They were yummy."

He turned his attention to Danna. He leaned forward and raised his eyebrows.

"Can you tell us what time Pete St. John's breakfast reservation is this morning?" Danna asked.

Mr. Perez leaned back, standing erect. "Well, he was scheduled the same time as you, seven-thirty. But he left unexpectedly in the middle of the night, at our Pittsburgh, Pennsylvania stop." He shrugged his shoulders, "He said something had come up."

***

Christmas Day supper at Grammy and Grandy's began promptly at two p.m. Alexis watched Momma and Grammy June place on the table enough food to feed a whole circus troop, including the animals. At least that's what Grandy Tony said.

On Christmas Eve, they had eaten light and then opened presents. Alexis got an American Girls doll, coloring books and much more. They ate sugar cookies in the shape of snowmen and candy canes and Christmas trees. Then just before her bedtime they got photo albums out and looked at Grandy and Grammy and Lexie's daddy when they were all young. Even Babe was a puppy in some of them.

Momma and Grammy talked and smiled, and laughed and there were some tears that they wiped off, but they kept turning the pages. Before they finished the first album Grandy Tony left for his study. Alexis smelled cigars. Yuck. They were worse than cigarettes.

On Christmas morning Alexis found the bicycle Santa had left. It had training wheels so she didn't have to wait to be older. And Santa brought ever so many Duplo blocks. There might be enough to build a castle. Grandy and Grammy said they would bring the bike with them when they drove out in February.

Momma put a slice of spiro-sliced ham on her plate, and mashed potatoes and other good stuff. Grandy Tony said a long Christmas Day grace that mentioned God and Jesus and everyone at the table, plus her daddy. She tried to pay attention the whole time, because praying was important. God was love. And so was Jesus.

Momma kept telling her to save room for dessert, but Momma had put enough food on her plate for a lion tamer and his lions. Alexis felt both guilty for wasting so much food, and proud she followed Momma's instructions to save room for dessert. After Momma and Grammy cleared the table, Grammy brought out a pumpkin pie and also pecan.

"And there's vanilla ice cream or whipped cream as a topper." She said.

Alexis wondered if she could have both. Before she could ask, the doorbell rang. Grandy Tony wiped his mouth and put his napkin carefully on the table. He had good manners. He got up and went to the door.

"Who could that be?" Grammy said.

Alexis shook her shoulders. She didn't know. She heard Grandy open the door. But she didn't hear any voices, though she did hear something.

"June, Danna, I think you better come to the door," Grandy said.

They got up and went to the door. Grandy didn't mention her so Alexis stayed put. But as they left, Alexis spoon did find the tub of whipped cream.

On the third spoonful Alexis clearly heard a tiny whining voice, and then high-pitched yapping. A puppy!

***

Danna arrived at the doorway with June. Tony pointed down to the porch. A cage rested there. In the cage a puppy pranced and waggled its tail—its whole behind really. Across the street an olive drab sedan stood with the engine running, a man opened the driver's side door. He looked at them, threw his hands in the air, and called out, "I don't know anything. I'm just delivering it as ordered," he said. "Merry Christmas." He slid in and drove off.

Alexis screamed in the other room. "A puppy! A puppy!" Her feet padded to the porch.

She dropped to her knees. "Oh, Momma! A puppy. It's my puppy. It's what I wanted. Can I open the cage?"

"No, Lexie, it's not ours." Danna watched her daughter stick her fingers through the cage. The puppy alternately licked and chewed Lexie's fingers, yelping and whining while it chewed. Lexie stuck her face up against the cage's metal squares. The puppy set to cleaning her face.

Tony pointed to the top of the cage. "A card."

An envelope was fixed to the iron of the cage by a red ribbon. Danna untied the ribbon and opened the envelope. Inside she found a card. When she opened the card, a smaller envelope slid out. As she began to read the card, June and Tony stood on tiptoes over her shoulder.

Dear Alexis,

Please accept this puppy as a gift this Christmas from the Ott and St. John children. Because of your father's heroism, I had my dad when I needed him most, Wendy got to know her father, and my little brother, David, who was born last summer ... well, he owes your father his life. We wanted to give you something you can love, and something which will remind you every day what a brave man your father was.

I know he is watching you from Heaven right now. And he is smiling.

Merry Christmas,
Morgan Ott, Wendy St. John, and little David

Danna held out her open palms and turned to June and Tony. June staunched tears. Tony watched Alexis with the puppy. Tony was smiling. Danna opened the smaller envelope.

Mrs. Grant — Danna,
I know this gift goes against what you and Lexie discussed. But your daughter is so very bright. I think she'll surprise you how quickly she learns the responsibilities of care and feeding. And if this doesn't work out, I'll make it right. I'll take her — the puppy, that is.

I'm headed back to Fort Riley on January third. Please contact me if you wish me to take the puppy, or you need help getting it back to Sioux City—I do have connections with a few military pilots, you know.

And Danna, I agree with Morgan. Dave is watching right now, and he's wearing that big cockeyed grin.

Warmest Christmas wishes,

Pete

P.S. Tell Lexie the puppy's a Cockerel Spaniard. Her name is Babe.

Danna folded the note and placed it inside the larger one. She would not cry. She would not look at Tony or June.

"Momma... please. Can I open the cage?"

"Yes, Lexie. Let Babe out to meet her new family."

Ye Merry Gentlemen

A Phil Morris Christmas Story

Christmas fell on a Monday in 1933. On Friday, the twenty-second, my secretary, Jill Freely, and I buttoned down the agency for the holidays. Oftentimes, a private investigator will have a busy caseload in December, usually domestic issues. This year had been slow, the Depression and all. My work with Chief Detective Myers, one of Kansas City's finest, had put Swenson the swindler away in Leavenworth for a dozen years, and I'd plugged a bad guy or two, but the rest of my caseload had been small potatoes, like spouse "A" cheating on spouse "B," and vice-versa.

Barring emergencies, Jill and I wouldn't return to our modest office until January second. Jill had picked up some eggnog at the grocer's on Walnut at lunch. I had livened it a bit with the help of the bottle of bootleg Jim Beam in my bottom left drawer. As we wrapped up year-end paperwork we shared our plans. Jill would spend time with her family—both parents living in town, and her big brother and his family were here for the weekend from Wichita.

"So what about you, Phil?"

"No family," I said.

"No family here?"

"No family anywhere. My folks are dead. An only child. I haven't seen my uncle and aunt in Seattle since my mom's funeral when I was seventeen."

"Gee, that must be rough this time of year."

"Not really." I didn't want to talk about it. And I didn't want Jill to go all sappy and sentimental on me. "Besides, I got my Labrador Sammy."

"Your dog, right?"

"He's more than that. He's my pal."

"The way you talk about him, he walks on water."

"Nope. But he sure as hell can swim through it." We both laughed. The eggnog might have been kicking in.

I told her I'd eat Christmas Day dinner with my landlady, Lucille, a widow, and a few of her friends. Lucille loved Sammy almost as much as I did, but I didn't tell Jill that part—Private investigators like me don't go soft on dames or dogs.

I had Jill take Henry, the Rawlston Building's elevator operator, a mug of the nog while I worked on expense statements from Swenson's swindle case. Both Jill and I would have done some major belt tightening in 1933 if it hadn't been for that one.

Jill returned wearing a shit-eating grin.

"What?" I asked.

"You shoulda seen the look on Henry's face when he tasted it."

I nodded. "Liked it, huh?"

"Very appreciative."

I sent Jill home a bit early. She had some family thing they did every year on the Friday night before Christmas.

Fiddling with the Motorola, I found a Christmas music radio program. I hummed and sang along as I worked. I was harkening some herald angels with the folks on the radio when I heard doorknob rattle.

It was Jill. Her car wouldn't start. I offered her a lift home, that is, if my old Plymouth would fire up in this cold. Jill set Henry's empty eggnog mug on her desk and then plopped unladylike in the chair across from mine. All bundled up, she looked swell with her cheeks rosy from the cold. She tapped her toes to a choral version of "Here We Come a Wassailing" as I filed away the paperwork.

I stood and donned my winter trench coat. "Ready."

She switched off the Motorola.

Henry brought us down to the lobby, a nog-induced holiday grin on his kisser. We gave him our season's greetings, and I had Jill wait in the lobby while I went out to see if my jalopy would cooperate.

It did. First crank, full choke, lots of grumbling and smoke. I pulled up Walnut and stopped in front of the Rawlston lobby. Jill came running out, her gait a combination of ingénue and Notre Dame fullback.

"Brrr. Turn on the heat."

I patted the dashboard. "This old girl doesn't do heat for at least five minutes." The Plymouth sputtered into sparse traffic. "Where to, doll?"

Jill didn't like to be called "doll." But sometimes I liked to raise her dander. This time, instead of dander I got a button-cute smile. She knew I was teasing.

"My folks place is on Union Hill. Head for 28th and Main."

I turned south on Main. "So what's the big family doings tonight?"

"Every year we have a light meal and some holiday cheer," she turned toward me, her left leg tucked underneath her. She knew how much I liked holiday cheer. "And then we walk our neighborhood singing carols. Several other families join us as we go."

Jill glowed as she spoke. "It's terrific fun. And the carolees, the ones we sing to, expect us. And they give us little treats, candy canes, donuts, things like that."

"Sounds like fun," I lied.

"Oh, Phil, it is. Even more fun than I make it sound."

We were both quiet for a few blocks. She turned to face the windshield, but that one bare leg remained underneath. At least that leg must have been warm, as the Plymouth's manifold heater was still missing in action.

"Say, why don't you join us?"

My noggin alarm went off, and my voice followed the noggin's directions. "No, I couldn't do that."

"Why not?"

"It's a family thing. I'd be an interloper." It was the first thing I came up with.

"No... I just invited you. I don't invite interlopers."

"Sorry, Jill, thanks for the kind offer, but I can't sing."

That twisted her back around to face me. "Nice try, but when my car wouldn't start I stood at the office door listening to you sing along with the radio. You have a fine voice."

Really? Was she kidding? My mother sang like an angel in Emporia's Methodist church choir, but my dad couldn't carry a tune from the kitchen table to the sink. When I was a kid, my teacher told me to sing very quietly. She didn't have to tell me twice, or say why.

"Nice try. But you're putting me on." I didn't look at her, my eyes fixed on the cross-traffic at Southwest Boulevard.

"False modesty doesn't become you, Phil."

"You're serious?"

"I am. Come on, it'll be fun."

New tack. "Nah, I got Sammy waiting at the apartment. It's past time for his walk, he's probably got his legs crossed." I didn't tell Jill my landlady takes him for a stroll every afternoon.

"Bring him along." She said, all bubbly and effervescent. "C'mon, let's go get him."

I hadn't anticipated that. We pulled through the intersection and continued south.

"Well?" The minx was persistent.

"There'll probably be other dogs. Sammy doesn't get along too well with other males."

She smiled. A pretty one. "Great then, it's settled. The only other dog who comes with us is Maizey, my folk's old female Cocker Spaniel. Let's go get Sammy. I'm anxious to meet this dog you're always talking about."

Trap sprung. I turned left toward the Paseo and my place.

***

Jill and Sammy hit it off like those peas in a pod. We took him for a quick walk, during which he darted around sniffing and peeing on things, then returning to Jill to make sure she watched and approved. His butt wagged his tail to beat the band. He made me think of that movie star Shirley Temple, always working to be cute, and seeking approval.

Back at the Plymouth I opened Jill's door and Sammy and leapt into the front.

"Sammy! Get in the back." He appeared to have gone deaf. "He's used to riding up front with me. Back, boy." I snapped my fingers. That usually did the trick, but of course he no longer heard or understood commands.

"That's okay," Jill said. "We can all ride up front. It'll be warm and cozy."

"You sure?"

"Yep. Scoot over you mutt," Jill said. And *that* Sammy heard.

Jill slid in, and Sammy circled between us before curling into a ball as tiny as a dog his size could accomplish. Before we traveled two blocks he uncurled and sprawled across Jill's lap—the lucky dog.

"Sammy. No." I snapped my fingers.

"It's okay," she said, stroking his neck.

"I don't want him to run your stockings," I said, which brought a merry "Ha!" from Jill.

"Like a girl could afford to buy stockings these days," she said.

I'd noticed she hadn't been wearing them lately. Why'd I say that? "Sorry. I wish I could pay you more."

She stopped stroking Sammy and put her hand on my shoulder. "Phil, I know how lucky I am to have a job, period. You're lucky to have one, too. We should both count our blessings."

I nodded. She was right. Her hand returned to Sammy. My shoulder felt the loss.

***

Jill's folks had a smallish, two-story shirtwaist home on McGee near 30th. They were tickled to meet "the boss." Her older brother, Eddie, peppered me with questions. Apparently I was the only private investigator he'd ever met. I worked the modesty bent to the hilt. All the while Jill grinned privately at me, knowing I enjoyed the attention.

Maizey and my pup got along immediately. After some initial anatomical sniffing they ran about in some kind of canine tag game, taking turns being the pursuer and pursuee. And Eddie's two little girls giggled their way from room to room behind them.

We sat down to a very light, almost Spartan meal. Times were tough. Clark, her father, said grace eloquently, all about what we have to be thankful for. He included me as one of those things. It hit me that maybe Jill's income helped keep this Freely mob treading water.

"Time for a little nip before we brave the cold," Clark said. He produced a fancy decanter filled with bright red liquid. With great flourish, Clark poured each adult a near-full wineglass. "Salud," he said, and then took a drink.

Everyone else held their glasses, but apparently they waited for me. I took a respectable swallow. Holy smokes! It tasted like cherry cough syrup and rubbing alcohol.

They all laughed at whatever expression was pasted on my mug.

"What are we drinking here?" I whispered, my vocal chords nearly burnt away.

Another laugh.

"Prohibition and Depression makes for strange bedfellows," Clark said. "This concoction has become a Freely specialty. It's cherry Kool-Aid mixed with home brew corn alcohol which I get from an old Army buddy in Marysville. Drink up, there's more. It'll not only grow on you, it'll grow hair on you."

So after we each choked down two glasses, and I had finished imagining pretty Jill with a hairy chest, we bundled up and headed out the door. Clark and the missus assured me Sammy would be okay without a leash.

It was already dark, but Eddie carried a lantern. And it was cold. Why hadn't I grabbed my gloves? The Freelys had a routine, a half dozen songs at each home. Some, but not all of the same songs. Every house got "O Holy Night" and "Jingle Bells." And the Freelys harmonized on the former like they'd practiced for years. Jill had a strong, beautiful voice.

The singing reminded me of childhood Christmases in Emporia. My mother had Christmas Cantata choir practice on Tuesdays beginning before Thanksgiving. She'd lug me along, and while the adults sang, my pals and I ran rampant—quietly—through the old church. The bell tower was a favorite spot to lurk. Those were good times.

The third home we caroled had a biscuit for Maizey, but hadn't anticipated Sammy. In a moment of Solomonic wisdom, the lord of the house broke it in half. Both dogs wagged vigorously at the compromise. Some teenagers from that place joined us as we trekked on.

I'd had my icy hands in my coat pockets for some time. On our walk to the next home, Jill placed her mittened hand into the crook of my arm. Funny how an insignificant gesture like that can take on great import. For just a moment I was a teenager again, glowing with the warmth of an adolescent crush. Sammy trotted along in front, almost tripping us, his expression was one of clear approval.

During our circuit the Freelys sang a new carol I hadn't heard before called "I Wonder as I Wander." It was a beautiful song, though it took me a couple of stops to pick up on it.

We were back on the Freelys' side of the street and nearly home when Jill's hand slid into my overcoat pocket and joined mine. Even through the mitten's heavy wool fabric she radiated warmth.

Our group had grown to nearly twenty by the time we completed the circuit. In the street in front of the Freelys' house we finished our caroling with a loud, rousing version of "God Rest Ye Merry Gentlemen," and then everyone repaired to their own homes.

Inside, we sat around the living room fireplace, the fire snapping and popping from pine logs. Mrs. Freely handed out mugs of undoctored eggnog. Without the punch of booze, the flavors of nutmeg, cinnamon, and clove stood out. Good stuff. Sammy and Maizey curled up together, toasting their fur near the hearth.

In my easy chair, I looked around at the Freely family. The two girls struggled to keep their eyes open. Eddie's wife curled on his lap in the chair across from me. On the davenport, Clark had one arm around each of *his* girls—wife Sharon, and Jill seated closest to me. Jill had a funny grin on her face. She had been watching me take the whole scene in.

"If Norman Rockwell were here, we'd be on the cover of *The Saturday Evening Post*," I said softly to her.

She closed her eyes and nodded as if she were imagining it.

As I finished the nog I took a gander at my father's old pocket watch. Though I had nowhere I needed to be, I felt it was time for Sammy and me to make our exit. I stood and stretched, arms reaching for the ceiling. Sammy joined me, his front end stretching low and hind end stuck up in the air.

"Mr. and Mrs. Freely, it was a pleasure meeting you. Thank you for including Sammy and me in your family celebration. Right, boy?" Sammy bashed his tail against the nearby easy chair.

We said our pleasantries, and Jill offered to walk us out to my Plymouth. She didn't put on a coat. There was no hand-holding as we walked, though she had wrapped her arms around herself to stave off the shivers. Gallantly, I put my arm around her. She leaned into me as we walked. Sammy trotted back and forth in front as if his sole purpose in life was to trip us.

"I had a swell time, Jill," I said at the car.

She rolled from my side around to face me. We hugged. "I'm glad you came—both of you," she directed at Sammy, who wagged with enthusiasm. Then she looked up at me, her arms still around my waist, her expression expectant, begging to be kissed.

I don't know what happened or why. I separated myself from her grasp, wished her a Merry Christmas, piled my dog and me in the car and drove off. Jill stood at the curb, hugging herself for warmth, an odd expression on her face.

I swear, if the Plymouth hadn't started on the first try I would have jumped out of the car and planted one on her. But it did and I didn't. As I drove home Sammy slept beside me. I replayed the scene over and over, wondering why I hadn't kissed her. Was it because I was her employer? I certainly was attracted to her. Yes, she was my employee. But more than that she was my friend. She was my confidant, my advisor, and my conscience.

Before we reached my place I vowed to Sammy, "I won't let another Christmas go by without kissing those lips."

Sammy raised his black brows as if to say, "I'll hold you to it, you numbskull."

Jack Kline, Author

Jack Kline's award-winning short stories and essays have appeared in numerous publications, including *Star Magazine, Kansas City Voices*, the popular *Chicken Soup for the Soul* book series, and United Kingdom's *Prole* magazine. A Kansas University Literature and Creative Writing graduate, and KU's Pee Dee Brown Creative Writing Award winner, Jack's collection of short stories, *Blowing Carbon*, was published in 2010.

Jack is perhaps best known for his private-eye novels, set in Kansas City during the Depression years. *But Not for Me* (2017) was his first novel. Expect a release of the followup novel, *Rhapsody*—which takes Phil, Rusty, Jill, and the gang into 1935—in early 2020.

Jack lives with his family, dogs and horses near Louisburg, Kansas, USA. And is proud to be known as an unabashed coyote lover. [Though his dogs may disagree.]

Made in the USA
Monee, IL
23 December 2019

19509701R00127